Holy Terrors

HOLY TERRORS

Thinking about Religion after September 11

BRUCE LINCOLN

THE UNVERSITY OF CHICAGO PRESS / CHICAGO AND LONDON

BRUCE LINCOLN is the Caroline E. Haskell Professor of History
of Religions at the University of Chicago. His books for the University
of Chicago Press include *Authority: Construction and Corrosion* (1994)
and *Theorizing Myth: Narrative, Ideology, and Scholarship* (1999).

The University of Chicago Press, Chicago 60637
The University of Chicago Press, Ltd., London
© 2003 by The University of Chicago
All rights reserved. Published 2003
Printed in the United States of America

11 10 09 08 07 06 05 04 03   1 2 3 4 5

ISBN: 0-226-48192-1 (cloth)

Library of Congress Cataloging-in-Publication Data

Lincoln, Bruce.
   Holy terrors : thinking about religion after September 11 / Bruce Lincoln.
      p.   cm.
Includes bibliographical references and index.
   ISBN 0-226-48192-1 (alk. paper)
      1. September 11 Terrorist Attacks, 2001.   2. Terrorism—Religious aspects.
3. Religion—Philosophy.   4. Religion and culture.   I. Title.
   BL65.T47 L56 2002
   291.1′787—dc21

                                                2002007099

⊗ The paper used in this publication meets the minimum require-
ments of the American National Standard for Information
Sciences—Permanence of Paper for Printed Library Materials,
ANSI Z39.48-1992.

For my mother
Gerry Grossman

CONTENTS

Parts of this book were written in the months after September 11, 2001, as I struggled to react in an intellectually responsible fashion to the immediate events and the broader, more complex issues that day raised. As a historian of religions, the most pressing item to ponder was the extent to which the attacks of September 11 could rightly be considered religious. My initial attempt involved a close reading of four key texts: the instructions that Mohamed Atta and others studied in the last days of their lives (chapter 1), speeches given by George W. Bush and Osama bin Laden as military action commenced in Afghanistan on October 7 (chapter 2), and the interpretations of September 11 offered by Jerry Falwell and Pat Robertson immediately thereafter (chapter 3). Exploring the religious aspects of their rhetoric and consciousness, however, meant confronting a much more general and considerably less tractable question: What do we mean by "religion"?

Over the years I have usually ducked that question, while gradually edging closer to it. Since the late 1970s I have focused much of my attention on a related issue that is only slightly less vast, that is, the changing roles religion has played (or can play) in politics and culture, above all in moments of violent struggle. I came to this set of interests at the time of the Iranian Revolution (1977–79), when I realized that theory then current among students of religion had very little to say about the world-historic events unfolding before our eyes: least of all, about the unexpectedly potent mix of the religious and the insurgent.

This book represents my attempt to think through the nature of religion, to identify its core components (discourse, practice, community, institution), and to specify its historically changing relation to other aspects of culture (particularly the ethical, aesthetic, and political). In the first three chapters, I consider several key texts immediately connected to the events of September 11. These are extreme, and not typical data, for the study of religion, but precisely for that reason I find them challenging, important, and analytically revealing. In chapters 4 through 6, I turn to other data and am particularly concerned with three moments, projects, and contexts. First, there is that which commenced with the Reformation and culminated in the Enlightenment, when Europeans, reacting to the horrors of the Religious Wars, reorganized their culture such that religion was consigned to a much-diminished role in culture. Second, the period of nineteenth- to twentieth-century colonial and neocolonial domination, when European and North American powers exported and sought to impose this minimalist model of religion on the rest of the world. Third, the reaction that gained force in the period after the end of the cold war, as activists throughout the globe sought to reassert religion's dominating position in culture against the preferences of postcolonial elites and the secular states they inhabit.

The chapters appear roughly in reverse order from that in which they were written. Thus, chapter 6, which treats revolutionary movements with a strong religious character, was written in the early 1980s, in the wake of the Iranian upheaval. Chapters 4 and 5, which treat the place of religion in culture and the question of why religious conflict has come to be so common in the postcolonial context, were written in the late 1990s, as patterns of violent struggle changed dramatically after the cold war era. Both of these pieces were substantially revised and updated after September 11. Chapters 1 and 2, which work out a general definition and theory of religion, while dealing with key documents relevant to the attacks of the 11th, were written in October and November of that same year. Chapter 3, which pursues some notorious reactions to the 11th, took shape in January and February 2002.

Various of these pieces were presented in oral form on one occasion or another, and I benefited greatly from the critical responses I received from colleagues at the Universities of Copenhagen, Colorado, and California at Santa Cruz (chapter 1); the University of Chicago and Yale University (chapter 2); the American Academy of Religion, Rocky Mountain Regional meetings (chapter 3); Bates, Dartmouth, and Reed Colleges and the University of California at Santa Barbara (chapter 4); Mount St. Mary's College and Århus University (chapter 5); and the University of Minnesota (chapter 6). In particular, I should like to thank Louise Lincoln, Saba Mahmood, Charles Hirschkind, and Martin Riesebrodt for reading and commenting on various pieces and, more broadly, for their ongoing collegial conversation and stimulation. I am also most grateful for the splendid assistance of Mari Rethelyi and Nathelda McGee and the ongoing support of Clark Gilpin and Rick Rosengarten. For various invitations, comments, feedback, provocation, and input, I am indebted to Stefan Arvidsson, Ron Breiger, William J. Buckley, John Calvert, Dipesh Chakrabarty, Ira Chernus, John and Adela Collins, Erik Davis, Robin Derby, Karen DeVries, Wendy Doniger, Prasenjit Duara, Roxanne Euben, Nancy Frankenberry, Roger Friedman, Armin Geertz, Cristiano Grottanelli, Donna Harraway, Richard Hecht, Christopher Hill, Greg Johnson, Joseph Jorgensen, Lansine Kaba, Vittorio Lanternari, Bruce Lawrence, Gary Lease, William Malandra, Margy Mitchell, Chandra Mukerji, Orlando Patterson, Hans Penner, Ole Riis, Kari Robinson, Mikael Rothstein, Erik Reen Sandberg, Seth Sanders, Jim Scott, William Shepherd, Jonathan Z. Smith, Jørgen Podeman Sørensen, John and Sara Strong, Tove Tybjerg, Jens Vanggaard, Matt Waggoner, Marilyn Waldman, Margit Warberg, Morten Warmind, Steven Wasserstrom, and Susan Zakin.

CHAPTER ONE

The Study of Religion in the Current Political Moment

I

Before we can begin to think about the ways religion, culture, and politics interact, either in general or with direct reference to the September 11 attacks, it is useful to have some clarity about what we take "religion" to be. Attempts to define religion, however, are presently in serious disarray. In the not-too-distant past, Clifford Geertz's view of religion as a "cultural system" was more or less hegemonic. The classic paragraph, on which a generation of students was trained, posits that

> a religion is (1) a system of symbols which acts to (2) establish powerful, pervasive, and long-lasting moods and motivations in men by (3) formulating conceptions of a general order of existence and (4) clothing these conceptions with such an aura of factuality that (5) the moods and motivations seem uniquely realistic.[1]

Within the last decade this formulation has fallen badly out of favor, largely as the result of Talal Asad's critique, which involves two telling points. The first proceeds from his observation that Geertz made interiority the locus of the religious (as indicated by his nouns: symbols, moods, motivations, conceptions). This works well for certain styles of religiosity: above all (and not coincidentally), Protestantism, which thus becomes the implicit model of religion per se. There are, however, things one intuitively wants to call "religion"—Catholicism and Islam, for instance—that are oriented less toward "belief" and the status of the individual believer, and more to embodied practice, discipline, and community.[2] Under Geertz's definition, such concerns and traditions tend to be ignored, distorted, rendered aberrant, or relegated to the margins of the religious.

The conclusion that Geertz unwittingly normalized features of his own (necessarily parochial) cultural/religious background is the starting point for Asad's second, more radical critique. Geertz's error, he argues, was not simply the product of some individual failing, but a specific manifestation of problems inherent to the project. For insofar as the task of defining anything presumes a discrete object that can be identified in contradistinction to others, this implies a model of "religion" that emerged only with the Enlightenment. Prior to that time, even in western Europe religion cannot be analytically (or practically) disarticulated from virtually all other aspects of culture.

As Peter Gay and others in his wake remind us, the Enlightenment can be read as a long struggle against the regime of truth that was centered in and championed by the medieval church. Weakened by the Reformation and Wars of Religion, the church and the faith it represented retained their connection to—and considerable control over—all aspects of social, political, intellectual, and economic life. The goal of those who waged this struggle (from Bayle to Kant, by way of Hume, Diderot, and Voltaire) was to constrain and deprivilege this hegemon, opening space for secular arts and sciences, not to speak of political economy.[3] Kant brought this struggle to an end with a compromise formulation, whereby "religion" was acknowledged as the only means to engage lofty metaphysical issues like the immortality of the soul, but inappropriate for all other matters. For everything save metaphysics, reason is both necessary and sufficient, and it is with this division of intellectual labor that Western modernity was founded.[4]

The view of religion as delimited, and therefore definable, is thus itself culturally bound, historically recent, and discursively loaded. "There cannot be a universal definition of religion," Asad concludes, "not only because its constituent elements and relationships are historically specific, but because that definition is itself the historical product of discursive processes."[5] And since he wrote his *Genealogies of Religion,* most have heeded his counsel.[6]

While the second part of Asad's sentence is wonderfully insightful, it is not clear to me why it entails the absolute prohibition of the first phrase. Is not all language "the historical product of discursive processes"? Granted, this makes language imperfect, elusive, and considerably more complex than common sense would have it. It hardly renders futile all efforts at definition, however, particularly when one understands these as provisional attempts to clarify one's thought, not to capture the innate essence of things. Returning to the specific question, one can begin to improve on past efforts by acknowledging, with Asad, that an atypical example—that is, the severely restricted religion advocated by Kant toward the end of the Enlightenment— got definitional efforts off the ground. Given this, the end result of our definitional labors ought to problematize, and not normalize, the model that prompted their inception. To this end, we need to stress two points. First, that which makes this delimited type of religion heuristically useful also makes it an extreme case: hardly the paradigm against which to measure all other examples. Second, when we take this as a starting point for discussion, we invert a line of historic development. Clearly delineated religions do not have this characteristic by "nature" but acquire it as the result of fierce historical struggles, in the course of which they suffer amputations and are forced to withdraw from their involvement in many other areas of culture (see further, chapter 4).

II

Differences in the extent to which the religious is imbricated with, or—to put it more strongly—penetrates and controls other aspects of culture, often become evident in moments of cultural contact. Consider, for example, a text written by Sayyid Qutb (1906–1966), an influential Islamist author and theoretician. Although he initially worked with the Free Officers who brought Gamal Abdul Nasser to power, Qutb later became disenchanted with Nasser's mix of nationalism and socialism, which he found secular and soul-less. Accordingly, he shifted his allegiance to the Muslim Brotherhood (Al-Ikhwan al-Muslimin), for which he was imprisoned from 1954 to 1964. Freed briefly, he took the opportunity to publish his most militant work, *Milestones* (*Ma'alim fi al-tariq*, also translated as *Signposts Along the Way* [1964]), which led to his rearrest and execution by hanging (August 29, 1966), notwithstanding protests throughout the Muslim world.

Prior to his imprisonment, Qutb was employed as an inspector of public schools by the Egyptian Ministry of Education. In the wake of the Second World War, he became increasingly critical of Westernizing trends, against which Egyptians needed to protect their "spiritual capital and intellectual heritage."[7] Between November 1948 and August 1950, a grant from the Ministry of Education let him study and travel in the United States, where his views deepened and became more critical.[8] Distressed by many aspects of American culture—from the violence of football to homeowners' obsession with lawn care (in which he perceived a retreat from social interchange and civic spirit)—Qutb was most concerned with the state he came to call *jahiliyyah* in his later writings. Traditionally, this term designates the age of spiritual ignorance characterizing the pre-Islamic period of barbarism, and he extended its usage to describe the modern world's malaise, where *jahiliyyah* was not just a matter of ignorance, but a more active state of rebellion against God's sovereignty on earth.[9]

Shortly after returning to Egypt, Qutb wrote about a church dance he observed in Greeley, Colorado, where he studied for a time at the Colorado State College of Education.[10]

> Every young man took the hand of a young woman. And these were the young men and women who had just been singing their hymns! Red and blue lights, with only a few white lamps, illuminated the dance floor. The room became a confusion of feet and legs; arms twisted around hips; lips met lips; chests pressed together.[11]

Qutb was not disturbed simply by the eroticism he took to be indecorous and improper.[12] More troubling, but analytically most revealing, was the enabling condition of this offensive spectacle: the disconnection between the preceding "religious" church service and the "social" event that followed, as is signaled by his gasp of horror: "These were the young men and women who had just been singing their hymns!" In a proper society, as Qutb saw it, people understood that God's law spoke decisively about relations between the sexes. In America such things seemed left to the whims of fashion and secular moral standards ("good taste"). Religion—such as it was—had been confined to a limited time, place, and role (Sunday mornings, bedtime prayers, Easter and Christmas), with little capacity to shape and stabilize other aspects of human activity or invest them with transcendent meaning. As he put it in the same essay, "No one builds as many churches as the Americans do. . . . Notwithstanding all this, there is no one as removed from feeling the spirituality, respect, and sacredness of religion than the Americans."[13]

One could unpack this incident at much greater length, but for the moment let me simply note that it is wrong to constitute Qutb as a representative of "Islam," which is no more a monolithic entity than is "American religion." One can find many Americans who sympathize with his view that religion ought to be the dominating force in society (cf. chapter 3), just as one can find many Muslims who feel religion need not control all aspects of life but can leave a certain space for relaxation and recreation. Qutb's activism, in fact, was prompted by his perception that *jahiliyyah* was sweeping through Egypt and was especially favored by elites of the secularizing postcolonial state (for a discussion of like situations elsewhere, see chapter 5).

The difference between Qutb and his Greeley hosts reveals two models of the religious that can probably be found in all religions, particularly those that encompass large numbers of people in diverse historic eras, geographic regions, and social strata. One style—that of Qutb—I would characterize as maximalist, rather than "fundamentalist," a term that has inflammatory connotations and fails to capture what is really crucial: that is, the conviction that religion ought to permeate all aspects of social, indeed of human existence.[14] The other, by contrast, is minimalist. This is the position taken by Kant at the culmination of the Enlightenment, which restricts religion to an important set of (chiefly metaphysical) concerns, protects its privileges against state intrusion, but restricts its activity and influence to this specialized sphere. Definition can begin with the more recently emergent minimalist type of religion but needs to be capacious and flexible enough to cover maximalist types and the long spectrum of intermediate positions. That said, we still need to consider what the constitutive elements of an adequate definition might be.

III

Before taking the leap, let us recall Asad's narrower objection to Geertz. Any definition that privileges one aspect, dimension, or component of the religious necessarily fails, for in so doing it normalizes some specific traditions (or tendencies therein), while simultaneously dismissing or stigmatizing others. Asad calls specific attention to the need to include both practice and discourse.[15] As he made clear, one also has to get beyond models that privilege interiority and understand that religious subjects are also bound in moral communities that enjoy their allegiance and serve as a base of their identity (thus, Durkheim). Further, communities are governed—sometimes more and sometimes less strictly—by institutional structures that direct the group and command their members' obedience (thus, Weber).

A proper definition must therefore be polythetic and flexible, allowing for wide variations and attending, at a minimum, to these four domains:

1. *A discourse whose concerns transcend the human, temporal, and contingent, and that claims for itself a similarly transcendent status.* Discourse becomes religious not simply by virtue of its content, but also from its claims to authority and truth. Astrophysicists, for instance, do not engage in religious speech when they discuss cosmogony, so long as they frame their statements as hypotheses and provisional conclusions based on experimentation, calculation, and human reason. The same is true when morticians describe what happens after death. But should they ground their views in Scripture, revelation, or immutable ancestral traditions, in that moment their discourse becomes religious because of its claim to transcendent

authority.[16] Insofar as certain propositions or narratives successfully claim such status, they position themselves as truths to be interpreted, but never ignored or rejected. Contestation then takes place within the realm of hermeneutics. Religious discourse can recode virtually any content as sacred, ranging from the high-minded and progressive to the murderous, oppressive, and banal, for it is not any specific orientation that distinguishes religion, but rather its metadiscursive capacity to frame the way any content will be received and regarded.

2. *A set of practices whose goal is to produce a proper world and/or proper human subjects, as defined by a religious discourse to which these practices are connected.* Religious practices, which generally divide into the ritual and the ethical, render religious discourse operational, moving it from the realm of speech and consciousness to that of embodied material action. As such, they have a transitive character, being the way discourse acts on the world, including the people through whom this action occurs. At the same time, they are reflexive in nature, being the way human subjects act on themselves in sustained projects of religiously motivated and informed programs of self-perfection. No practices are inherently religious, and any may acquire a religious character when connected to a religious discourse that constitutes them as such. Thus, for instance, for a man to grow a beard becomes a religious action when he does so in emulation of Jesus or the prophet Muhammad, constituted as the ultimate examples of human perfection. Lacking an argument and motive of this sort, his beard reflects a strictly aesthetic preference.

3. *A community whose members construct their identity with reference to a religious discourse and its attendant practices.* Those who revere the same texts (whether written or oral), adhere to the same precepts (taken from those texts and their commentaries), and engage in the same sorts of practices (grounded in texts and precepts) have a great deal in common. Even when they disagree with one another, their disagreements are framed by reference points on which they can concur: How is this Scripture to be interpreted? When (and how) should that ritual be performed? What is the best response to a given behavior that shared values define as a moral failing? All of this creates the basis for strong sentiments of affinity that are also fostered by specific aspects of discourse and practice, like regular assemblies for worship, prohibitions on intermarriage with outsiders, or threats of excommunication for various infractions. Individual and col-

lective identities come to be embedded in groups that are bound together in this fashion. Borders, simultaneously social and religious, hold members of one group separate from those whose beliefs and practices differ sufficiently that they can be marked as other. Even seemingly trivial differences—those of diet and dress, for example—can assume enormous import in the construction of alterity. But the fact is, these are hardly trivial, for practices understood to be governed by sacred injunctions constitute the observant as faithful and righteous, radically different from nonobservant outsiders, who are constituted as neither.

4. *An institution that regulates religious discourse, practices, and community, reproducing them over time and modifying them as necessary, while asserting their eternal validity and transcendent value.* Coherence over space and continuity over time are secured by formal or semiformal structures staffed by officials, experts, and functionaries authorized to speak and act not only on behalf of the community, but also on behalf of the tradition or religion itself. Such structures vary tremendously in their size, power, rigidity, elite status, funding, degree of centralization, degree of hierarchy, and style of operation. But in whatever form they take, they house the leaders who assume responsibility for preservation, interpretation, and dissemination of the group's defining discourse; supervision of its rituals; adjudication and enforcement of its ethics; nurturance, defense, and advancement of the community. Sometimes they derive considerable wealth from such service, and they are regularly caught up in serious contradictions. The most important of these is the contradiction between their own corporate self-interests and those of the community, and that between the need to accommodate change while preserving claims to eternal truth.

All four domains—discourse, practice, community, and institution—are necessary parts of anything that can properly be called a "religion." Each can be developed and emphasized to differing degrees and can relate to the others in various ways. Discourse and practice may be closely coordinated, for instance, or badly out of sync (for all that members of the community or officials of the institution desperately claim otherwise). Similarly, institution and community may cooperate closely, with the latter subordinate to and directed by the former, or may be locked in power struggles and hold each other in contempt. Institution may value discourse above practice and community, just the reverse; or they may agree on the value of practice, while differing on the specific practices they valorize. Further, every macro-entity that gets called a "religion"—Buddhism, Islam, or Christianity, for example —has countless internal varieties and subdivisions, each of which undergoes its own historic process of development and change.

Sweeping characterizations of these macro-entities are always misleading, especially the simplistic caricatures that contrast one to another ("Protestantism is strong on discourse; Catholicism, on practice," to take a cheap example). At best, one can try to assess specific movements or tendencies within a tradition at given moments of their development, recognizing that each macro-religion encompasses many such groups and tendencies. No one of these is normative; rather, they compete with one another—sometimes sharply—with the capacity to represent themselves as most faithful, authentic, or orthodox being both an arm and a stake of their struggle (see further, chapter 6).

IV

With this by way of background, I want to consider a document of extraordinary historic importance: the set of instructions Mohamed Atta left in his luggage on the morning of September 11, 2001, along with his last will and testament, apparently intending that these papers be found after his death (appendix A).[17] Two other copies of these same instructions were found in the effects of hijackers on other planes, which suggests that, at a minimum, these were provided to the leaders of each team, who used them to prepare for—and understand—their deeds of September 11.[18] Although these documents bear no signature, authorship is best attributed to the apparatus responsible for the attacks, presumably the al Qaeda network. Close reading permits one to see how religious discourse construed mass murder and terrible destruction as religious practices and also affords insight into the way al Qaeda constitutes itself as a religious institution that acts on behalf of a broader religious community (the Islamic *ummah*).

The text begins with formal invocations, one quite orthodox ("In the name of God, the most merciful, the most compassionate," §1) and one almost shockingly unconventional ("In the name of God, of myself and of my family," §1). After this it segues into prayer, prompting the reader to ask forgiveness for all his sins (something that would be granted a martyr [*shahid*]) and to view the coming events as deeds done to glorify God (§1). Having thus gestured toward the immediate future, the text recalls a moment from the paradigmatic past, which it frames as the model for what is to come: "Remember the battle of the prophet . . . against the infidels, as he went on building the Islamic state" (§2).

The balance of the text is organized in three sections and describes how to prepare for the coming operation. A few paragraphs treat technical matters (§§3, 4, 15), but the overwhelming majority address spiritual concerns. Even those items explicitly identified as "worldly things" (§16) are invested with religious significance, as when the men are told to wear tight-fitting clothes "since this is the way of the pious generations after the Prophet [who] would tighten their clothes before battle" (§16).

Along these lines, the first paragraph of the text's first section ("The Last Night") includes suggestions that have struck uninformed readers as banal, profane, or pedestrian: "Shave excess hair from the body and wear cologne. Shower" (§3). In the last paragraph of the same section, however, cleansing one's body is described as ablution: a ritual act of self-purification that helps secure salvation.

> Pray the morning prayer in a group and ponder the great rewards of that prayer. Make supplications afterwards, and *do not leave your apartment unless you have performed ablution* before leaving, because *the angels will ask for your forgiveness as long as you are in a state of ablution,* and will pray for you. (§17; my emphasis)

In general, the hijackers' last night on earth is treated as a time for spiritual preparation, during which they should pray for success, victory over their enemies, also for God's mercy and assistance, making use of specific prayers at appropriate times and places (§§7, 8, 10, 13, 17). In addition, they should read and reflect on the Quran, especially two suras that treat battles against nonbelievers: suras 8 and 9, which are explicitly commended in §5 and repeatedly cited thereafter (§§6, 21, 22, 28, 30, 33). Mere reading, however, was not enough. Verses of the Quran were to be spoken into cupped hands, then rubbed into one's body and equipment so their power could be quite literally incorporated (§14). The men were to review their plans (§4), check their equipment (§15), anticipate problems that might arise (§11), and calm themselves with the knowledge that paradise was near (§§6, 9, 10, 11; cf. §§23, 24, 25, 30, 36). Most sweepingly, the text advises: "Purify your soul from all unclean things. Completely forget something called 'this world.' The time for play is over and the serious time is upon us" (§9).

The section titled "The Second Step" treats the interstitial period between leaving home on the morning of September 11 until entry into the plane. Driving to the airport, the men should "remember God constantly" (§18) and thereafter offer a series of prophylactic prayers every time they enter new space or terrain (§§18, 19, 23, 26). Implicitly acknowledging the anxieties they will experience, the text counsels its readers to master fear, which it defines as a great form of worship appropriate only for God (§§21, 22). Time and again it promises victory and paradise, effortlessly mixing Quranic allusions with reassurance of God's support.

"The Third Phase" treats events inside the plane, beginning with the prayer one offers at the threshold. Once seated, the men were to run through all their prayers once more, keeping "busy with the constant remembrance of God" (§27; cf. §§28–29). Finally, the text discusses the violence needed to seize the plane and the ethical problems posed by these bloody acts. It admonishes that killing is to be done without anger (§32) and ought not cause pain (§31), while insisting that no prisoners be taken (§33) and no compassion ought to compromise the mission (§31). Two arguments are provided not simply to justify, but to sanctify the shedding of blood. The more frequent, predictable, and important of these is citation of Muhammad's military practices as a legitimating and inspirational model (§§29, 32, 33, 37). More original—and more shocking—is the constitution of the hijackers' first victims (i.e., the flight attendants) as sacrificial beasts, whose throats would be slit in ritual fashion (§31; cf. §15).

Imagining the moment when its readers have taken control of the planes, the text envisions a short time for congratulations, when one could cite appropriate verses from the Quran, sing an inspirational song, and sip water as minimal reward for a job well done (§§34, 35). After which, comes the finale.

> When the hour of reality approaches . . . wholeheartedly welcome death for the sake of God. Always be remembering God. Either end your life while praying, seconds before the target, or make your last words: "There is no God but God, Muhammad is His messenger." (§35)

V

If we consider this text and its relation to the events of September 11 with reference to the four categories discussed earlier, it is convenient to begin with practice. The instructions rarely treat the mission as a whole and never mention its fiery finish. Instead, the operation is atomized, decomposed into a series of minute actions, each of which is invested with religious significance in one fashion or another. Thus, bathing is treated as ablution and connected to purifying one's soul (§§3, 9, 17). Dressing is represented as girding for battle, with care to preserve modesty, and follows the model established by the first Muslims (§16). Tying one's shoes has the same significance attached to it (§16), while all items of one's equipment—luggage, clothes, knife, papers, and personal effects—are to have prayers physically embedded in them (§14). Riding in a taxi becomes an occasion to remember God, with separate supplications for entry and leaving (§18–19). Stepping into the plane is experienced as part of "a battle for the sake of God" (§27), and the instant the plane begins to move, one should pray "because you are traveling to Almighty God, so be attentive on this trip" (§27). In similarly maximalist fashion, sharpening one's knife is preparation for a ritual of sacrifice (§15); gritting one's teeth, a repetition of gestures used by the first Muslims (§29), as is singing songs to boost morale (§34). Throughout their mission, the men are counseled, "Be busy with the constant remembrance of God" (§27). Further, "You must remember to make supplications wherever you go, and anytime you do anything, and God is with his faithful servants" (§26).

The text effectively instructs its readers how to overcome whatever hesitations might interfere with their mission. Acknowledging the possibility of fear, doubt, and moral qualms (§§6, 9, 11, 21, 22, 24, 31, 37), it offers a program of exhortation and reassurance to those on the brink of terrifying acts. Indeed, its goal is to close whatever gap might remain between the ideals al Qaeda advocates and their full realization in these men. "Do not seem confused or show signs of nervous tension," it counsels. "Be happy, optimistic, calm, because you are heading for a deed that God loves and will accept" (§24; cf. §§6, 14, 29). This last phrase concisely summarizes the text's persuasive project: definition of the entire undertaking—theft of the planes, murder of their crews, and the final paroxysm of death and destruction—as something religiously sanctioned: "a deed that God loves and will accept."

That task is accomplished by welding practice to discourse: providing each grubby, banal, or lethal act with authoritative speech that ennobles and redefines it not just as a moral necessity, but also a sacred duty. Three different bodies of discourse are used in this fashion. The first is that of the text itself, which mobilizes and encapsulates the others. Its authorial persona having been effaced, it manifests impersonal certainty and fervor, speaking a language drenched in piety, through which it purports to make the divine will patently apparent. God himself is mentioned a full eighty-nine times and appears in more than three-quarters of the document's paragraphs (30 out of 38). Mentions of the Prophet and the first generation of Muslims are also frequent (25 times in 15 paragraphs), and hardly a paragraph goes by without discussion of such topics as purification (5 times), martyrdom (5 times), the need to struggle against infidels (11 times), or the promise of heavenly reward (6 times).

Second, there is prayer, the discourse—also the practice—that connects the human to the divine through the medium of language. In nine different paragraphs, the text enjoins prayers or supplications appropriate to the following occasions: evening (§§7, 13), morning (§13, 17), when entering a car (§18), when entering a town (§§13, 18), when entering a new place of any sort (§§18, 19), when in motion (§26, 27), before meeting the enemy (§13), for victory (§§7, 28), and at the moment of death (§35). Once again a maximalist intention is evident in the desire for religious devotion to fill all time, space, and action, maintaining unbroken one's connection to God and calling forth his reciprocity.

> You must remember to make supplications wherever you go, and anytime you do anything, and God is with his faithful servants, He will protect them and make their tasks easier, and give them success and control, and victory, and everything. . . . (§26)

Finally, there is the most privileged discourse of all: that of the Quran, which the instructions implicitly claim to mediate, while parasitically appropriating as much of its authority as possible. No fewer than twenty-two Quranic quotations appear in this text and many more allusions. No doubt is permitted concerning the divine status of Scripture, since citations are invariably introduced as God's word (§§6, 11, 12, 17, 19, 20, 21, 22, 27, 28, 30, 33, 34, 37).[19] Most emphatic is the following formulation:

> Remember God frequently, and the best way to do it is to read the Holy Qur'an, according to all scholars, as far as I know. It is enough for us that it is the words of the Creator of the Earth and the plants, the One that you will meet [on Judgment Day]. (§8)

Shrewd use of Quranic citations also permits the instructions to blur the present moment with paradigmatic events of the past. Regularly, the passages the text chooses to quote describe the first generation who heeded the Prophet's call and took up arms to defend the new faith (§§12, 21, 28, 30, 33, 34, 37). These fervently committed Muslims overcame enemies far more numerous than they (§§12, 37), and their victory is attributed to God's support, with the result that power is redefined as a function of piety rather than wealth, arms, or numbers.

This point is made in several passages to which the instruction text gives double emphasis. These are found in the two chapters of the Quran that the text commends as proper reading for the "last night" (§5). Having insured that the men would have read these passages and would understand their original context, the text then quotes key phrases from them in ways that connect their contents to the bold actions planned for September 11. Thus, in discussing the hijackers' approach to the airport, the text takes up the question of American technical superiority. "All of their equipment and gates and technology will not prevent, nor harm, except by God's will," it explains. "The believers do not fear such things. The only ones that fear it are the allies of Satan, who are the brothers of the devil" (§21). Then it goes on to quote a Quranic phrase, by way of reassurance: "'so fear them not, and fear Me, if you are believers'" (§21). This comes from a passage that says nothing about technology but thematizes the conflict as one of believers against unbelievers.

> Fight the leaders of unbelief . . .
> *Are you afraid of them?*
> *You would do better to be afraid of God,* if you are believers.
> Fight them, and God will chastise them at your hands
> And degrade them, and He will help you
> Against them, and bring healing to the breasts of a people who believe.[20]

VI

In like fashion, the text redeploys familiar and evocative Quranic terminology to construct al Qaeda's chosen adversary not in terms of national, racial, or political alterity, but as people to whom one is opposed on strictly religious grounds. They are infidels (§§2, 28), nonbelievers (§§22, 30, 32), and allies of Satan (§21), while the text construes its readers and authors as believers (§§19, 21), the faithful (§§12, 27), allies of God (§22), and God's faithful servants (§§26, 37). Over the course of its discussion, the hijackers gradually merge with the pious heroes who made possible Islam's initial triumphs and become their reinstantiation (§§2, 16, 29, 32). Conversely, the United States becomes the contemporary incarnation of *jahiliyyah:* the barbarism and spiritual ignorance that preceded Islam and offered savage—but misguided and unsuccessful—resistance to the Prophet, his armed followers, and his message (fig. 1.1).

Al Qaeda thus implicitly represents itself as the most faithful heir to the Prophet and his original followers, also the implacable enemy of savage nonbelievers. Seemingly strong, the latter are actually weak and will be defeated,

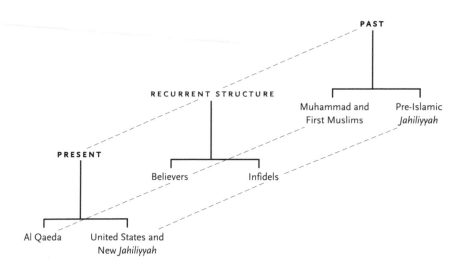

FIGURE 1.1 Alignment of contemporary struggles with those of the early Muslim era.

as were their *jahili* ancestors. Such a view picks up on the analysis advanced by Sayyid Qutb in his last, most radical writings, where he argued that a new and more virulent *jahiliyyah* introduced by the West had made powerful inroads within Islam. To counter that trend, restore proper religion, and rescue the world from its own most profane impulses, he argued that a small group of the faithful would have to withdraw from the corrupt world in a repetition of Muhammad's Hegira. From safe redoubts, they could prepare to meet and overthrow the *jahili* order, with confidence in God's support. Compounding his earlier maximalist views with a new militance, he thus produced blueprints usable for a group like al Qaeda.

> *Jahiliyyah* always takes the form of a living movement in a society and has its own leadership, its own concepts and values, and its own traditions, habits, and feelings. It is an organized society and there is a close cooperation and loyalty among its individuals, and it is always ready and alive to defend its existence consciously or unconsciously. It crushes all elements that seem to be dangerous to its personality.

> When *jahiliyyah* takes the form not of a "theory" but of an active movement in this fashion, then any attempt to abolish it and to bring people back to Allah would be useless if it presented Islam merely as a theory. Since *jahiliyyah* controls the practical world and has a living and active organization for its support, mere theoretical efforts to fight it cannot even be equal to it, much less

superior. When the purpose is to abolish the existing system and to replace it with a new system which in its characteristic principles and all its general and particular aspects is different from the controlling *jahili* system, then it stands to reason that this new system should also come into the battlefield as an organized movement and a viable group. It should come into the battlefield with a determination that its strategy, its social organization, and the relationship between its individuals should be firmer and more powerful than the existing *jahili* system. . . .

Islam's theoretical foundation—the belief—therefore must be actualized in the form of an organized and active group from the very beginning. This group must separate itself from the *jahili* society and become independent and distinct from the active and organized *jahili* society whose aim is to block Islam. The center of this new group should be a new leadership, the leadership which first came in the person of the Prophet himself, peace be on him, and after him was delegated to those who strove to bring people back to Allah's sovereignty, authority and laws. . . . The Muslim society cannot come into existence simply as a creed in the hearts of individual Muslims, however numerous they may be, unless they become an active, harmonious, and cooperative group, distinct by itself, whose different elements, like the limbs of a human body, work together for its support and expansion, and for its defense against all those elements that attack its system. This group must work under a leadership that is independent of the *jahiliyyah* so it can organize its various efforts in support of one harmonious purpose, and strengthen and widen the Muslims' Islamic character in order to abolish the negative influences of *jahili* life.[21]

VII

By associating itself with the first generation of Muslims in the fashion urged by Qutb, the al Qaeda network conceived itself as a militant vanguard institution, mounting counteroffensives on behalf of the Muslim community. That community, in their view, had been weakened by the influence of savage nonbelievers, whose ways are debased and irreligious. Overcoming them becomes possible only as the vanguard recovers and revives the proper Islamic faith, by grounding all practice—indeed, all existence—in the sacred discourse revealed by God through his prophet.

Finally, we are ready to consider the morning of September 11. No prose can capture the events of that day or the emotions they occasioned. No analysis can soften the impact of steel in flight with tall, but vulnerable towers. No attempt at interpretation can quell one's anguish and sorrow for the thousands buried in the rubble.

It is tempting, in the face of such horror, to regard the authors of these deeds as evil incarnate: persons bereft of reason, decency, or human compassion. Their motives, however—as revealed by the instructions that guided their final days—were intensely and profoundly religious.[22] We need to take this fact seriously, uncomfortable though it be, since it can tell us important things about the events of the 11th, the broader conflict of which those events are a part, and also the nature of religion. For if there is one thing they make abundantly clear, it is that religion and ethics are not indivisible.[23] Rather than being a divine and unfailing ground of morality, religion begins with a human discourse that constructs itself as divine and unfailing, through which deeds—any deeds—can be defined as moral. It was their religion that persuaded Mohamed Atta and eighteen others that the carnage they perpetrated was not just an ethical act, but a sacred duty.

The religion in question was not a monolithic entity that can be labeled "Islam." Rather, these men embraced an extremely militant reformulation of maximalist currents within Islam. To be sure, there are those who consider this style of Islam—which others have styled "Islamist"—to be Islam proper, and who polemically characterize all other styles as adulterations and perversions of one sort or another. But we need not repeat that error, any more than we must accept their view of the West—America, above all—as monolithically minimalist and utterly debased in its style of religiosity.

This construction has roots in Qutb's *Milestones* (1964) and can be traced a bit further to Hasan al-Banna, who founded the Muslim Brotherhood in 1928, and Abul Ala Mawdudi, who founded the Jamaat-i-Islami about 1941.[24] More recently, as American power has impinged ever further on the Muslim world, resentment has grown, along with a more aggressive discourse that constitutes the United States as the antithesis of Islam and of religion in general. In that discourse America becomes the Great Satan, a monstrous entity responsible for a global flood of impiety and profanation, as witnessed in the blatant sexuality and random violence of the popular culture it so happily (and profitably) exports.

I want to suggest not only that Mohamed Atta and his comrades understood America in these terms (that much is clear enough), but also that their view found expression in the targets they chose: the Pentagon and World Trade Towers, central emblems of American military and economic might. I also think the minimal armaments they carried—a few knives and box cutters—have more than technical significance. Indeed, the assailants' technological impoverishment constitutes a sign to be read and may well have been meant to be so.[25]

In effect, these men drew a stark contrast between themselves and those they attacked, dramatizing the differences between two ideal-types of society and culture. As men of unshakable faith, armed only with the most humble tools, they presented themselves as metonymic images of a people whose strength lies in their religion, to which all other concerns—economy, politics, technology, and the rest—are distinctly subordinated. The buildings against which they hurled themselves are likewise tropes for a people preoccupied with money, machines, and armies, but shockingly unconcerned with religion.

In their authors' intentions, the events of September 11 thus constituted an experiment for all to behold, testing two different types of society and two different types of power. To put it more precisely, they measured the relative power of two antithetical cultural formations, as seen from an Islamist perspective: Islam (+ religion/− all else) versus America (− religion/+ all else), in a showdown encounter. The results were instantaneously relayed throughout the globe, thanks to the technology and communications network of the latter party. Predictably, those results were read in different fashions, reflecting the predispositions of the readers, but many surely took the hijackers' success as a sign of God's favor.

In the United States, September 11 was immediately associated to Pearl Harbor and condemned as a sneak attack perpetrated by cowards and villains. While hideously destructive, it was not a knockout blow, but one that alerted a sleeping, peaceful giant to a terrible danger. Once roused, that giant could be counted on to marshal its forces and wage a relentless campaign to rid the world of this evil. The analogy has its points, particularly in its sense of a resilient America under attack, but it also has its problems. Chief of these, I think, is its disinterest in the attackers' intentions. In December 1941 the Japanese general staff meant to deliver a definitive first strike that would end the war with a single blow by crippling American military capacities. Those who planned and executed the attacks of September 11 can hardly have expected to do anything on that order.

Rather, as I have suggested, their goal was to make a point: to demonstrate that, all appearances to the contrary notwithstanding, they possessed a power infinitely superior to their adversary's and of an entirely different order. In contrast to the imperial Japanese, the Islamists designed their assault more for sign value than use value.[26] Their point was not so much to kill people, destroy buildings, and shatter defenses (although their results along these lines were hardly negligible), but to show the world how awesome was the form of power they—and they alone—possessed. From the perspective of those who executed the attacks, September 11 was meant to avoid the Japanese mistakes of 1941. Not Pearl Harbor: they were meant to be Hiroshima. That is to say, a spectacular event in which sign value and use value supported each other and were meant to display power that was not only overwhelming and decisive, but unprecedented and incomparable. Those who suffered such attacks were presumably meant first to surrender and thereafter to refashion their culture after that of the victors.

CHAPTER TWO

Symmetric Dualisms: Bush and bin Laden on October 7

I

On Sunday, October 7, 2001, less than a month after the attacks of September 11, President Bush announced the American military response in a televised address (appendix B). Within hours there came a riposte from Osama bin Laden, who had prepared a videotape in anticipation of such military action and conveyed it to the widely viewed Arabic language network al-Jazeera, with instructions that it should be released shortly after Bush's broadcast (appendix C).

Within the Muslim world, the bin Laden tape met an enthusiastic reception, and it presented many Westerners with their first sustained, relatively unmediated view of this man. Although his language and self-presentation were primarily aimed at a Muslim audience, bin Laden's charisma was still evident, even to a Western audience relatively unfamiliar with the cultural codes on which he drew and relatively unsympathetic to the arguments he offered. Given that the tape showed him as articulate in his speech, coherent in his views, passionate in his commitments, also able to rebut Bush on certain points and to highlight others the president chose to ignore, it complicated attempts to demonize him. Treating control of the airwaves as a military objective, the Bush administration quickly prevailed on American TV networks not to broadcast any further tapes from bin Laden. Rather, they should limit themselves to excerpts only, accompanied by "appropriate commentary" by responsible journalists, who could be counted on to tell the desired story. Government officials also pressured print media to adopt similar policies.[1]

The censorship thus imposed effectively deprived most Americans of the opportunity to hear bin Laden and to improve their regrettably slim and shallow understanding of this man: his grievances, goals, dreams, and delusions; his relative degree of rationality, as compared to the genuinely monstrous qualities of his *ressentiment*.[2] Further exposure might make him all the more repugnant to American audiences or might enhance his charismatic aura, but it would surely help create a better-informed public: the basis of any democratic society and the proper ground from which policy ought to

emerge. Although the administration has voiced fears about providing opportunities for propaganda and the transmission of coded messages to un-
derground operatives, officials are clearly uncomfortable with anything that
might permit a nuanced perception of bin Laden and create sympathy for
him on any point. Far better to keep him a cartoonish stereotype of Oriental-
ist fantasy: the "Mad Mullah," a wild-eyed, turbaned, and bearded fanatic,
whose innate irrationality precludes taking him seriously but makes him a
serious danger.[3]

   If in the future we will hear bin Laden only in snippets carefully chosen
and packaged for our consumption, it becomes all the more important to listen closely—and critically—to his tape of October 7, for it is a subtle, complex rhetorical performance and a revealing piece of evidence. The same can
be said of President Bush's speech. Indeed, it is useful to study the two texts
in tandem, for they show unexpected similarities, as well as instructive
differences.

II

Both men constructed a Manichaean struggle, where Sons of Light confront
Sons of Darkness, and all must enlist on one side or another, without possibility of neutrality, hesitation, or middle ground. Bin Laden stated that the
events of September 11 produced a radical estrangement and categorical division between two rival camps. His discourse, moreover, helps construct
and exacerbate that division, as does the broader discourse in which he par-
ticipates, which helped shape practices culminating in the 11th. "I tell them
that these events have divided the world into two camps, the camp of the
faithful and the camp of infidels. May God shield us and you from them"
(§9). Bush made the same point in the central paragraph of his text, pressing
a complex and variegated world into the same tidy schema of two rival
camps. The orienting binaries of this structure—good/evil, hero/villain,
threatened/threat—are much the same for Bush as for bin Laden, but, predictably enough, he assigned the roles in opposite fashion. "Every nation has
a choice to make. In this conflict, there is no neutral ground. If any government sponsors the outlaws and killers of innocents, they have become outlaws and murderers, themselves. And they will take that lonely path at their
own peril" (§12).

   Bin Laden's pronouncement "May God shield us and you from them"
(§9) is particularly revealing for the way it establishes (and manipulates) relations among four entities, three of them marked by pronouns. Two of the
pronouns—"us" and "them"—are set in opposition to each other, and the

third ("you") is suspended between these two parties. The task this text takes for itself is to draw that "you" into close association with "us" and away from the enemy "them." It does this by aligning the sole noun of the phrase and its transcendent marker unambiguously with the "us": "May God shield us—and you—from them" (§9). In similar fashion, but working with different symbolic codes, Bush tried to discourage support for the enemy by consigning any would-be sympathizers to perdition: "And they will take that lonely path at their own peril" (§12).

To nail down the negative side of his binary structure, the president denounced his adversaries—not just the bombers of the September 11, but any government associated with them—as outlaws, murderers, and killers (§12). In other passages he called his adversaries "barbaric criminals" (§9) who harbored "evil plans" (§6). For the most part, however, his favored term was "terrorists," a phrase repeated so often in his and in common parlance that its meaning has come to seem transparent and its appropriateness self-evident (§§1, 2, 5, 6, 9, 10, 13). Still, it is worth specifying the semantics of what has become the key signifier in our contemporary political discourse. As a rule, it is reserved for nonstate groups (often, but not necessarily, Islamist) who use violence, including surreptitious attacks against civilians and others, to advance political goals that pit them in opposition to state structures, policies, and ruling elites.

There are, however, some telling exceptions that reveal how loaded this terminology is. The Contras in Nicaragua, for instance, also RENAMO in Mozambique, UNITA in Angola, and the Mujahedin in Afghanistan when Afghanistan was Soviet-controlled all met the requirements of the above definition. But having been created by the CIA as proxies to harass regimes that incurred American disfavor, they could hardly be called "terrorists" in official parlance. Rather, "our" terrorists were usually dubbed "freedom fighters" when they had to be acknowledged: a term bin Laden, his al Qaeda network, and numerous other groups locked in struggle against powerful states would also surely claim for themselves.

Like Bush, bin Laden was also relentless in his use of a key signifier to denounce and demonize his enemies. His term of choice was "infidels," which he repeated five times in a relatively short address (§§3, 6, 8, 9, 11). The Quranic resonances of this word were useful to him, as was its literal denotation ("unbeliever," "enemy of the faith"). In bin Laden's usage, however, it acquired a more specific and pointed contemporary referent, designating non-Muslim states that project their military, political, economic, and cultural power into spaces Muslims regard as most holy. These "infidels" include, above all, the United States, whose stationing of troops in Saudi Arabia (home to Mecca and Medina) has been a prime concern of bin Laden's since the 1991 Gulf War (§§10, 11).[4] More recently, he had begun to make similar points regarding the American-backed Israeli presence in Palestine, home of Jerusalem, Islam's third most sacred city (§§3, 4, 11).[5]

The moral failings bin Laden attributed to infidels include vanity (§6), arrogance (§1), and duplicity (§7), along with callous and wanton violence (§§4, 5, 7). Their offenses also consistently have a religious character, since they not only violate Islamic law, but are actively directed against Muslims and the Islamic community. President Bush is thus "the head of international infidels" (§§6, 8), America "the modern world's symbol of paganism" (§8), and for many decades Americans have been "killers who toyed with the blood, honor and sanctities of Muslims" (§4). Accordingly, in the opening words of bin Laden's text, September 11 is construed as nothing less than the visitation of divine vengeance on a sinful nation: "Here is America struck by God Almighty in one of its vital organs, so that its greatest buildings are destroyed. Grace and gratitude to God" (§1; cf. §4).

III

While most of the characters who inhabit the two texts are noble heroes, outrageous villains, or waverers called to choose between these two rival camps, there is another set of cardboard figures whose features are equally determined by their propagandistic utility. This consists of children in danger who are menaced by one side and protected by the other.[6] Bush evoked such images in three passages. In the first and most straightforward, he spoke to the situation of "the starving and suffering men and women and children of Afghanistan" (§7). Notwithstanding the fact that he was bombing their country, he portrayed American action as directed against a political regime and a terrorist apparatus, not the Afghani people. The bombings were "carefully targeted actions" (§2) directed against military targets, specifically "al Qaeda terrorist training camps and military installations of the Taliban regime" (§1; cf. §6). To the suffering people of the country, and above all the innocent children, he promised airdrops of food, medicine, and supplies as a token of American friendship. "The oppressed people of Afghanistan will know the generosity of America and our allies" (§7; cf. §8).

In a second passage Bush began by gesturing toward traditional associations of America with "freedom" (an evocative and polyvalent signifier that deserves more attention than is possible here), then quickly dilated this notion. By the time he was finished, he had positioned the United States as champion of freedom throughout the globe, hedge against darkness, and protector of the weak. In this context he conjured up the specter of frightened children. "We defend not only our precious freedoms, but also the freedom of people everywhere to live and raise their children free from fear" (§14).

Having dealt with starving Afghani children and frightened children in foreign lands, Bush returned to address the situation of American children in the least successful passage of an otherwise deft rhetorical performance. This was the cloying paragraph toward the conclusion of his address, in which he cited a letter he received "from a 4th-grade girl, with a father in the military. 'As much as I don't want my Dad to fight,' she wrote, 'I'm willing to give him to you'" (§21). The other children Bush described had entered his narrative only as objects: objects of suffering, pity, fear, and terrible circumstances far beyond their control; objects who had been worked on by evil others to their detriment; and objects to be worked on in the future by a moral, sympathetic American self, concerned to restore their well-being. This American girl was different, however. Although threatened by menacing forces herself, she responds as a subject in ways Bush offered as a model of how proper Americans do and ought to behave: courageous, self-sacrificing, and resolute (also utterly unquestioning of their leaders).

Bin Laden's concerns for children were more local and more pointed, being most immediately focused on the plight of Iraqi children who are deprived of food, medical supplies, and sometimes also their lives by the American embargo, which has now lasted for more than a decade. Relatively little discussed in the West, this issue occasions deep concern in the Middle East, where it is often taken to reveal the cruelty of which Americans are capable and the double standard they employ in their dealings with Muslims. Bin Laden takes this analysis one step further. By connecting the Iraqi embargo to the specter of Hiroshima and Nagasaki, he charges the United States with war crimes and crimes against humanity, while subtly inserting racism in the indictment. For it would seem that Americans are capable of such atrocities only when their enemies are nonwhite. "They have been telling the world falsehoods that they are fighting terrorism. In a nation at the far end of the world, Japan, hundreds of thousands, young and old, were killed and this is not a world crime. To them it is not a clear issue. A million children in Iraq, to them this is not a clear issue" (§7).

Could bin Laden have anticipated that Bush would represent himself as a protector of children? If so, his emphasis on the Iraqi young amounts to a further charge of hypocrisy. Pressing to make the most of this, he hyperbolically overstated the extent of their sufferings. However credible or incredible one might find his figure of a million victims (§4), the Iraqi children became a trope for the situation of all Muslims, whose weakness has exposed them to Western aggression, particularly in the last century. The indictment bin Laden leveled also had a double edge to it. Aimed at the United States in the first place, it landed on Muslim leaders who have failed to speak out against the embargo, in the second. "A million innocent children are dying at this time as we speak, killed in Iraq without any guilt. We hear no denunciation, we hear no edict from the hereditary rulers" (§4). Against this background, bin Laden positioned himself and his followers as the most courageous and righteous defenders of their people: "those [who] have stood in defense of their weak children" (§3).

IV

For all that Bush and bin Laden both represented themselves as righteous protectors of the weak, the two men projected very different types of authority. Bush's is official and governmental, grounded in elections, laws, and the Constitution of a nation-state. In truth, it is probably misleading to regard Bush as an individual speaker, and this for two reasons. First, he surely was not the author of his address in any conventional sense. Rather, he read a text coauthored by unnamed members of his staff. The words themselves were theirs as well as his, and he spoke as the representative and director of this apparatus. Second, and much more important, he spoke in his official capacity as head of state, representing the state and, beyond that, the nation. Or, to put it more precisely, the American state spoke to the American nation through him as its representation and conduit.

In partial acknowledgment, but also partial concealment of these intricacies, Bush began his address by alluding to the state authority vested first in his office and second in his person ("Good afternoon. On my orders the United States military has begun strikes" [§1]). At two other points, he made explicit reference to his title and office, proudly placing himself among American presidents (§13) and commanders in chief (§18). Noting that he spoke "from the Treaty Room of the White House, a place where American Presidents have worked for peace" (§13), he was surrounded by flags as he defined the struggle in terms of his nation's traditional ideals. These center on peace (mentioned four times in §13, including the assertion "We're a peaceful nation"), justice (especially in his charge to the troops, "Your goal is just" [§20; cf. §6]), and freedom (mentioned four times in §14 and used, somewhat lamely, to euphemize the mission: "The name of today's military operation is Enduring Freedom").[7] Two of these values recur in his final clarion cry, "Peace and freedom will prevail" (§23), and the third is probably implicit. No American call to arms is conceivable without enumeration of these cardinal virtues, but of particular analytic interest at present is their distinctly secular nature.

In contrast, the authority bin Laden claimed is religious and charismatic. The chief ideal he voiced is faith, and he spoke of his group as "the camp of the faithful" (§9; cf. §3), whose victory may be expected, for "the wind of faith is blowing" (§10). As leader of the faithful, he claimed no formal titles or office but presented himself as a holy warrior (*mujahid*), seated on a prayer rug, with Kalashnikov and Quran close at hand. At times his discourse bordered on the prophetic, although Muslim doctrine recognizes Muhammad as the last prophet and bars anyone since from claiming such status.[8] In truth, bin Laden spoke very little of himself, submerging his own identity in the first-person plural via an "us" he defined as "the group that refuses to be subdued in its religion" (§6).[9] More menacingly, he described the hijackers of September 11, with whom he implicitly claimed connection (while not actively taking responsibility for their acts), as "a group of vanguard Muslims, the forefront of Islam," whom God has blessed "to destroy America" (§3).

v

As a religious leader, bin Laden sought to mobilize a following that cuts across all political distinctions of citizenship, also all ethnic and other potential lines of cleavage, uniting all Muslims without exception on the basis of their shared faith. "Every Muslim must rise to defend his religion" (§10). Shared faith also implies a shared perspective, grounded in shared experiences and born of a common history. In bin Laden's account, that history breaks into three periods: (1) a time of Islamic grandeur, which ended with the dissolution of the Ottoman Empire and the caliphate in the aftermath of the First World War; (2) a time of suffering, shame, and victimization by Western powers, which lasted from 1918 until September 11, 2001; and (3) a period just commencing, introduced by the Islamist counterattack on the West, launched on September 11. This is announced toward the beginning of his speech: "What America is tasting now is only a copy of what we have tasted. Our Islamic nation has been tasting the same for more than 80 years of humiliation and disgrace, its sons killed and their blood spilled, its sanctities desecrated" (§§1–2; cf. §4).

If bin Laden aspired to mobilize all Muslims on the basis of their religion, ignoring their identities as citizens of different nation-states, Bush's approach was precisely inverse. The prime group he sought to rally consisted of American citizens, regardless of their religious affiliations (§§13–18, 21–22).[10] Beyond that, he portrayed himself as having assembled an alliance of religiously diverse states, support from whose leaders ratified his actions and policies, thereby confirming that these were based in shared human values, not the particular self-interest of one powerful state. "We are supported by the collective will of the world" (§4; cf. §§3, 7, 10). To that end, he kept religious language to a minimum and took special pains to assure this was not a latter-day Crusade.[11] Rather, he represented himself and America as both well disposed to Muslims. "We are the friends of almost a billion worldwide who practice the Islamic faith" (§8).[12]

Just as Bush labored to refute any constructions of the conflict as a war of Christians against Muslims, so bin Laden attempted to preempt inverse constructions of it as a struggle against "terrorism." "They have been telling the world falsehoods that they are fighting terrorism. In a nation at the far end of the world, Japan, hundreds of thousands, young and old, were killed and this is not a world crime. To them it is not a clear issue" (§7). One gets the impression of fencers or chess players trying to anticipate and parry the other's favored lines of attack. Were one to press the game metaphor, it would be necessary to explore the competitors' different styles, bin Laden's being much more ferocious, impassioned, and unpredictable, Bush's more plodding and cautious. This is less a difference between two personalities than between the two types of authority Max Weber described as charismatic and official-bureaucratic.

VI

Although one might expect that the religious nature of his persona, vision, and language might limit him to a vaporous, mystic, or otherworldly discourse, bin Laden was actually quite concrete in identifying his chief grievance. Thus, while the president's rhetoric remained at the level of inspiring but vague generalizations (freedom vs. terrorism), in his closing paragraphs bin Laden adapted his equally lofty (and equally inflammatory) formulations to signal more immediately pragmatic issues. "The wind of faith is blowing and the wind of change is blowing to remove evil from the Peninsula of Muhammad, peace be upon him" (§10). Then, expanding the discussion to include Palestine, he made the same point again. "I swear to God that America will not live in peace before peace reigns in Palestine, and before all the army of infidels depart the land of Muhammad" (§11). Clearly, removal of American troops from Muslim holy lands—Saudi Arabia, above

all, and Palestine in the second place—remains his prime and most immediate goal.

The American government surely does not want to yield on this demand,
given that the troops stationed in Saudi Arabia help keep a friendly, if highly
corrupt and unpopular regime in power, which secures the continued supply
of cheap oil from Saudi fields in return. One should not underestimate the
importance of this concern for an administration filled with oilmen, from
the president and vice president on down. There are also principled reasons
why one would refuse the demands of blackmailers. But the administration
has also been concerned not to acknowledge any construction of the conflict
as a struggle over scarce resources (oil, above all) or as a violent reaction to
American policies many Muslims find offensive, lest this confuse the American public and sap national resolve. It is for this reason that Bush finds it
best to maintain a strictly dualist narrative of civilization versus terrorism
and good versus evil.

Others clearly prefer the variant, but equally dualistic construction provided by Samuel Huntington's "clash of civilizations," where the adversaries
are identified as the (Judeo-Christian) West versus Islam.[13] Although one
might expect Bush to find this congenial, the fact that he has avoided incorporating it in his public statements (except as an occasional subtext) shows
that he—or at least his staff—is aware of its potential dangers. In truth, it is
bin Laden who benefits from constituting the struggle as one of Islam versus
the West, and it is he who propagates such a view. American interests are better served by models that permit Muslim nations to enlist—or at least stay
neutral—in a moral, but not religious campaign: one that pits civilization per
se against all that is *uncivilized,* that is, "terrorism," "fanaticism," and "evil."[14]

VII

The speeches of Bush and bin Laden mirrored one another, offering narratives in which the speakers, as defenders of righteousness, rallied an aggrieved people to strike back at aggressors who had done them terrible
wrongs. For his part, Bush preferred to define the coming struggle in ethico-
political terms as a campaign of civilized nations against terrorist cells and
their rogue-state supporters. Bin Laden, in contrast, saw it as a war of infidels
versus the faithful. As a corollary, the two also differed in their willingness to
couch their views in religious terms, and this was probably the sharpest di-
vergence between them.

In the twelve paragraphs of his speech, bin Laden named God seven
times (§§1, 3 [2 times], 5, 9, 11, 12), from his opening assertion "Here is Amer-

ica struck by God Almighty" (§1) to his final benediction "God is the greatest and glory be to Islam" (§12). At other points bin Laden swore before God (§11), took refuge in God (§5), and called upon God for protection (§9), vengeance on enemies (§5), and a promise of paradise (§3). Throughout, his discourse is saturated in religiosity, as quantitative tabulation confirms. Of the 584 words he uttered, a full 101 are plainly religious (17%), not to speak of many phrases with subtler Quranic resonance.[15]

In the sharpest possible contrast, Bush made very little use of language that was unambiguously religious. Of the few times he mentioned religion directly, he tended to so with reference to the faith of others, for which he expressed tolerance and respect. There were two such examples. One was his claim "we are the friends of almost a billion worldwide who practice the Islamic faith" (§8). The other, his characterization of those responsible for September 11 as "barbaric criminals who profane a great religion by committing murder in its name" (§9). Beyond that, only three of his 970 words (.3%) were explicitly and exclusively religious. One of these conveyed his assurance that American presidents pray before sending troops to war (§18). The other two are found in the words with which he concluded his address. "May God continue to bless America" (§23). Much can be said about this phrase, and I will return to it shortly. In addition, there are some ambiguous phrases, in which one can hear religious resonance if one is so inclined: "evil plans" (§6), for instance.[16] But whatever one makes of these, the concentration of overtly and emphatically religious content in bin Laden's speech was almost sixty times greater than in Bush's.

VIII

We have seen that a prime purpose of bin Laden's address was to construct the conflict along religious lines, pitting Muslims—"every Muslim" (§§6, 10) and "our Islamic nation" (§2)—against infidels. But he also identified a second, internal class of enemies. These are the people he referred to as "hypocrites," by which term he designated those postcolonial state elites in Muslim nations who cooperate with Americans, help advance and protect their interests, and profit from this service (on which, see further, chapter 4). These are the people who failed to denounce the Iraqi embargo (§4), failed to speak out in support of Palestine (§3), failed to protest the 1998 American bombing of Afghanistan and Sudan (§8), but were quick to object when al Qaeda took up arms against the infidels (§§3, 4, 8). Notwithstanding his calls for pan-Islamic solidarity, bin Laden's rhetoric identified and exacerbated a sharp cleavage between those he would characterize as good and bad, or as I would have it, maximalist and minimalist, Muslims. For him, al Qaeda represents proper Islam, consisting of "those [who] have stood in defense of their weak children" (§3), "the group that refuses to be subdued in its religion" (§6), and "the forefront of Islam" (§3). The hypocrites, in contrast, are "apostates" (§5), camp followers of the infidels (§§3, 8), and persons estranged from the sufferings of their Muslim brethren (§4).

In a climactic passage, bin Laden called down God's judgment on such people. "The least that can be said about those hypocrites is that they are apostates who followed the wrong path. They backed the butcher against the victim, the oppressor against the innocent child. I seek refuge in God against them and ask him to let us see them in what they deserve" (§5). While he did not name the specific "hypocrites" he had in mind, they surely include the rulers of countries like Egypt, Jordan, Kuwait, and Saudi Arabia: that is, those whom the West prefers to call "moderates." Bin Laden faults such people severely for their failure to connect Islamic discourse with their political practice and seems to suggest that the Islamic community (*ummah*) ought to be led by institutions committed to maximalist positions and militant practice. Conceivably, extant states might reform themselves in this fashion, or, that failing, leadership should fall to a group like al Qaeda itself. The threat implied in the last phrase of his proclamation—"I seek refuge in God *against them*" (§5)—is real, if implicit. It amounts to a call for divine judgment to manifest itself in popular uprisings against those regimes that compromise Islamic solidarity by siding with the West in the war now beginning. It was lodged most immediately—and most credibly—against General Parvez Musharraf, who, under intense diplomatic pressure, agreed to help fight "terrorism" and permitted the American military to use air bases in Pakistan.[17]

If bin Laden's core contradiction involved the admission that politics was important as well as religion, Islam not being unitary, as religious ideals would have it, but also lacerated by political divisions, Bush's came on similar ground. Having consistently sought political unity and denied the religious aspects of the conflict in order to avoid the possibility of fragmenting his coalition along religious lines, he was ultimately forced to acknowledge the importance of religion in subtle, but revealing ways. Pressure for this came not only from Christian conservatives, a core part of his constituency, but also a broader resurgence of popular piety, as marked by displacement of the national anthem with the strains of "God Bless America."

While it has long been conventional for American presidents to close their speeches—particularly those that have some degree of solemnity—with the same tagline of "God bless America," this is not an idle or insignificant gesture. Rather, it attempts to reconcile two fundamental contradictions. The first of these involves the inevitable and irresolvable tension between a secular state (under its Constitution debarred from religious matters) and a nation that places strong value on its religious commitments. Second, within the religious nation, there are further unresolved tensions between Christian and pluralist models of the nation, as well as minimalist and maximalist constructions of its religiosity. "God bless America" says enough—just enough—to satisfy most factions, while offending no one gravely, save hardcore secularists.

"May God continue to bless America" (§23), however, goes beyond the conventional formula, and as such is linguistically marked. It suggests Bush and his speechwriters gave serious thought to the phrase and decided to emphatically reaffirm the notion that the United States has enjoyed divine favor throughout its history, moreover, that it deserves said favor insofar as it remains firm in its faith. Although those so inclined may dismiss Bush's closing words as obligatory, gratuitous, and virtually devoid of meaning, others will recognize them as the tip of a vast subtextual iceberg. While brief, they provide sufficient reassurance that American policy is rooted in a faith so profound it need not be trumpeted.

IX

Two brief flights of imagery stand out in an otherwise unembroidered text, and these helped Bush assert the religious nature of the conflict in the same moment he sought to deny it. Toward this end, both images contain biblical allusions plainly audible to portions of his audience who are attentive to such phrasing, but likely to go unheard by those without the requisite textual knowledge. Thus, his statement "the terrorists may burrow deeper into caves and other entrenched hiding places" (§6) reduced his adversaries to hunted animals, but also gestured toward a climactic scene of the Apocalypse. This is the moment when the Lamb of God (i.e., Jesus in his character of eschatological hero and avenger) opens the sixth seal on the scroll of doom, as described in the Revelation of Saint John 6:15–17:

> Then the kings of the earth and the great men and the generals and the rich
> and the strong, and every one, slave and free, hid in the caves and among the
> rocks of the mountains, calling to the mountains and rocks, "Fall on us and

hide us from the face of him who is seated on the throne, and from the wrath of the Lamb; for the great day of their wrath has come, and who can stand before it?"

This vision of evildoers hiding in caves and trying to escape God's judgment associates American bomb runs with the wrath of the Lord. At the same time, this passage from the New Testament indexes one from the Hebrew Bible: Isaiah 2:10–11, which addresses the unfaithful directly.

> Enter into the rock, and hide in the dust
> From before the terror of the Lord, and from the glory of his majesty.
> The haughty looks of man shall be brought low,
> And the pride of men shall be humbled;
> And the Lord alone will be exalted in that day.[18]

In similar fashion, Bush's statement that anyone who sides with bin Laden "will take that lonely path at their own peril" (§12) conjures up a host of biblical passages that contrast a path of righteousness with one of perdition. Among these, one can note Job 8:13 ("Such are the paths of all who forget God; the hope of the godless man shall perish") and Isaiah 59:6–8.[19]

> Their works are works of iniquity, and deeds of violence are in their hands.
> Their feet run to evil, and they make haste to shed innocent blood;[20]
> Their thoughts are thoughts of iniquity,
> Desolation and destruction are in their highways.
> The way of peace they know not, and there is no justice in their paths;
> They have made their roads crooked, no one who goes in them knows peace.

Biblical allusions may also be perceived in several of Bush's more trenchant phrases. "Killers of innocents" (§12) surely gestures toward Herod's slaughter of the innocents in Matthew 2 and perhaps also to Exodus 23:7 ("Do not slay the innocent and righteous, for I will not acquit the wicked"). Similarly, "there can be no peace" (§13) invokes the refrain of Jeremiah and Ezekiel: "They have healed the wound of my people lightly, saying 'Peace, peace,' when there is no peace" (Jeremiah 6:14, 8:11, 8:15, 14:19; Ezekiel 13:10, 16; cf. also II Chronicles 15:5 and Isaiah 57:21).[21]

These allusions provide a thunderous moral condemnation running parallel to Bush's more prosaic characterizations of the enemy as outlaws, murderers, criminals, and terrorists. The biblical subtext is not redundant, however. Rather, for those who have ears to hear, these allusions effect a qualitative transformation, giving Bush's message an entirely different status. This conversion of secular political speech into religious discourse invests otherwise merely human events with transcendent significance. By the end, America's adversaries have been redefined as enemies of God, and current events have been constituted as confirmation of Scripture.[22]

These allusions are instructive, as is the fact that Bush could only make these points indirectly, through strategies of double coding. Along with Bush's closing benediction, his biblical references acknowledge a serious cleavage within the American public and address those Americans who could be expected to reject the religious minimalism that otherwise characterizes his text. Far from denouncing them as improper Americans, however—the way bin Laden treated his "hypocrites" as bad Muslims—Bush provided reassurance for these people. Enlisting the specialized reading/listening and hermeneutical skills they cultivate, he encouraged them to probe beneath the surface of his text. There, sotto voce, he told them he understands and sympathizes with their views, even if requirements of his office (also, those of practical politics) constrain him from giving full-throated voice not just to the religious values they prefer, but to their maximalist construction of *all* values as religious.[23]

CHAPTER THREE

Jihads, *Jeremiads, and the Enemy Within*

I

Although the Arabic term *jihad* is commonly understood to denote a "holy war," its etymology and its full range of semantics are both better served by translation as "struggle."[1] In fact, two very different forms of struggle are spoken of as *jihad*, and these correlate to a categorical distinction of prime importance that is simultaneously spatial and moral.

Islamic doctrine conventionally divides the world into two contrasted domains. One includes all places where rulers have established a system of law based on the divine principles God revealed through the prophet Muhammad, and in which a community devoted to those principles constitutes the dominant majority. Such territory is referred to as the "Realm of Peace," and within this favored space, Muslims are enjoined to wage a constant struggle (*jihad*) against their own selfishness, laziness, and other shortcomings that inhibit their pursuit of religious self-perfection. The rest of the globe— which is to say, anywhere these principles have not yet been secured—is designated the "Realm of War" (*dar al-harb*). Here the struggle of *jihad* is not internal to the striving subject. Rather, it takes the form of aggressive military campaigns designed to spread the practices, laws, sensibility, and political structures that ground themselves in the Prophet's revelation, as mediated through Quranic text and authoritative oral traditions (*hadith*).

As aggressive campaigns of this sort succeed in winning territory, the Realm of War (*dar al-harb*) shrinks, while its positive counterpart expands. The ultimate goal is that day when the latter encompasses all the earth, at which time there will be no further need for the bellicose *jihad*: only the inner struggle of religious self-fashioning will remain. At that moment the Realm of Peace will be established in all its glory, or—to give it its Arabic name—the *dar al-Islam*, for *Islam*, which is cognate to the Arabic *salaam* and Hebrew *shalom*, means nothing other than "peace."

Given that the signifier "Islam" has also come to designate a specific religion (in the sense outlined in chapter 1), this word has a tendentious ambiguity built into it. As a result of easy slippage between the two sides of its usage, an idealized state ("peace") is equated (either explicitly or by implication) with a specific body of religious discourse and practice, as well as the community and institutions associated with them. The quasi-paradisal Realm of Peace may thus be understood as that space where the religion of Islam is hegemonic, and conversely, the hegemony of Islam is construed as the fulfillment of God's purpose. From the same perspective, any loss of territory to non-Muslims—as happened with the Spanish Reconquista, Ottoman reversals in the Balkans, the Soviet takeover of Afghanistan, the fate of Kashmir upon the partition of British India, and the Zionist establishment of Israel—is not just a military and political defeat, but an affront against God and an undoing of Islam in both senses of the word. For wherever such defeats have been suffered, the Realm of Peace (*dar al-Islam*) reverts to the Realm of War (*dar al-harb*).

II

Formulations of this sort are hardly unique to Islam. Indeed, they characterize—also motivate—many aggressive and expansionist projects. By way of comparison, we could cite the Crusades, European colonization of the New World, America's sense of "Manifest Destiny," or the religio-political dualism of the Achaemenian kings. Beyond their very real differences, all these historic projects drew their energies from sharp binary distinctions between "us" and "them," in alignment with other discriminatory contrasts, including moral/immoral, sacred/profane, modern/primitive, and dominant/submissive. Those who employ such discourses typically construe themselves as persons who understand and strive to realize God's will (or who strive to maintain the cosmic order, or at least to impose that order they define as rational and progressive), while characterizing their opponents as religiously ignorant and/or rebellious. The effect is to cast those against whom they direct their violence as persons who need their direction and chastisement.

All of this is clear enough. But notwithstanding the starkly dualistic categorization, systems of this sort contain complexities and obscurities that provide considerable room for maneuver. Groups constituted as "us" are nowhere near so monolithic in actuality as ideology and rhetoric would have it. And where some part of that "us" differs uncomfortably from the representation a given speaker provides for the whole, the consequent tension and instability can be handled in numerous ways. Blurring of differences is a classic and relatively mild response, as is defining those differences as unthreatening variations within an encompassing whole. A more contentious strategy is to define those who might be regarded as coreligionists or fellow citizens, but with whom one differs on a point deemed crucial, as outsiders to the community or, alternatively, traitors within. More radically still, such people can be represented as rebels against the divine order of which the community is the instantiation, thereby constituting them as a danger to God and community alike.

We have already seen one example of such operations in Osama bin Laden's denunciation of those he branded "hypocrites" (*al-munāfiqīn*), a term appropriated from the Quran and redeployed to telling purpose. Suras 9:73 and 66:9 group such persons alongside non-Muslims or infidels (*al-kuffār*) and enjoin the Prophet to struggle (literally, to wage *jihad*) ruthlessly against both of them.[2] Sura 3:161–62 describes the "hypocrites" as a group of Muhammad's early adherents who deflected his call to arms with a lame excuse, "saying with their mouths that which never was in their hearts." Charges of cowardice, betrayal, and deceit thus cling to the term. Neither infidels nor Muslims proper, the hypocrites occupy an interstitial position disdainfully characterized by the Quran as "nearer to unbelief than to belief."[3]

In speaking of the Saudi royal family and the ruling elites of other Muslim nations as "hypocrites," bin Laden alluded to these Quranic texts, thereby associating his enemies with those who were only fair-weather friends of the Prophet. Unwilling to wage the military struggle necessary in the Realm of War, their lies and excuses showed they were also incapable of waging the internal struggle requisite in the Realm of Peace. Placing himself in something approximating the role of the Prophet, bin Laden dismissed them as unworthy of trust, at best very imperfect and incomplete members of the Muslim community.

Bin Laden's rhetoric may be dismissed as a transparent attempt to define those with whom he disagrees as God's enemies, but one must still understand that he arrived at this tendentious conclusion by strictly religious means. Thus, when considering persons and situations in the present, he interprets them as contemporary instantiations of paradigms known from texts that he—like all Muslims—constitutes as a sacred reservoir of timeless truths. Cynical and principled aspects of this operation inevitably coexist, as do the political and the religious (if indeed one can separate these). What we have is a situation of mutual mediation, in which the actor's temporal situation of interest provides the lens through which he consults the canonic, putatively timeless text. Simultaneously and conversely, bin Laden's prior familiarity with the text—and the sedimented familiarity of others, which he experiences as an interpretive tradition—provides the lens through which he understands and responds to his situation.

III

Similar operations are also a staple of American religions. To take an obvious example, consider the notorious remarks the Reverend Jerry Falwell made on September 13, 2001, when he appeared on the *700 Club,* hosted by the Reverend Pat Robertson. Most dramatic—and most discussed—was the following tirade.

> JERRY FALWELL: And, I know that I'll hear from them for this. But, throwing God out successfully with the help of the federal court system, throwing God out of the public square, out of the schools. The abortionists have got to bear some burden for this because God will not be mocked. And when we destroy 40 million little innocent babies, we make God mad. I really believe that the pagans, and the abortionists, and the feminists, and the gays and the lesbians who are actively trying to make that an alternative lifestyle, the ACLU, People For the American Way, all of them who have tried to secularize America. I point the finger in their face and say: "You helped this happen." (§12)[4]

Clearly, Falwell—a well-known televangelist, founder of the Moral Majority, and longtime stalwart of the religious right—was relishing the opportunity provided by the attacks of September 11 to flog his familiar enemies.[5] Such broadsides are hardly unusual for him and his fellow televangelists, but when People for the American Way posted a transcript of the *700 Club* discussion (appendix D), nationwide outrage followed. Comment was widespread and almost entirely negative. Typical was the statement issued by Lorri Jean, executive director of the National Gay and Lesbian Task Force: "The terrible tragedy that has befallen our nation . . . has its roots in the same fanaticism that enables people like Jerry Falwell to preach hate against those who do not think, live, or love in the exact same way he does. The tragedies that have occurred this week did not occur because someone made God mad, as Mr. Falwell asserts. They occurred because of hate, pure and simple."[6]

Among the more gentle rebukes was that of President George W. Bush, who received indispensable support from Falwell and Robertson throughout his career, above all during the primary and general election campaigns of 2000.[7] Even so, the president was forced to turn on his erstwhile benefactors. When White House spokesman Ken Lisaius was asked about Bush's view of the Falwell diatribe, he offered a carefully worded statement: "The president believes that terrorists are responsible for these acts. He does not share those views, and believes that those remarks are inappropriate."[8]

Initially, Falwell tried to stand by his words, and Robertson—president of the Christian Broadcasting Network, head of the Christian Coalition, and 1988 candidate for president—offered his guarded support.[9] Upon realizing their position was untenable, however, Robertson quickly distanced himself, while his bumbling colleague made a series of reluctant and awkward attempts at apology and/or explanation. Falwell began backtracking in a phone call to CNN on September 14, in which he said, "I would never blame any human being except the terrorists, and if I left that impression with gays or lesbians or anyone else, I apologize."[10] At the same time, he reasserted his view that secularization and sin have "created an environment which possibly has caused God to lift the veil of protection which has allowed no one to attack America on our soil since 1812." This statement echoed points both he and Robertson made during the broadcast, when they spoke of how God "continues to lift the curtain and allow the enemies of America to give us probably what we deserve" (§8). Falwell said he came to his opinion "as a theologian, based upon many Scriptures and particularly Proverbs 14:23," although this was, in fact, a miscitation that reveals his haste and disarray.[11] Regarding the question of just which sins—and whose—had caused God to withdraw his protection, Falwell reiterated what he said on the program (§§10, 12, 14). The culprits remained the ACLU, People for the American Way, and other organizations "which have attempted to secularize America, [and] have removed our nation from its relationship with Christ on which it was founded."[12]

By September 17 Falwell released a much fuller statement, entitled "Why I Said What I Said," once again mixing retractions and reassertions in contradictory fashion. Although he shifted his discourse to the first-person plural, the same villains remained transparent, for all that "they" were now encompassed by "us": "We have expelled God from the public square and the public schools. We have normalized an immoral lifestyle God has condemned. American families are falling apart. Because of our national moral and spiritual decline during the past 35 years, I expressed my personal belief that we have displeased the Lord and incurred his displeasure."[13]

The difference between this formulation and Falwell's original use of the third person is more than semantic.[14] The latter posits two radically separate groups, a good one for whom the speaker takes his stand and a bad one against whom he thunders. Using the first-person plural makes both sides part of the same nation, all of whom share the same dangers. Although Falwell played with the notion that both factions share responsibility for their situation, he did so in an inconsistent, not to say a disingenuous, fashion.[15] Superficial gestures notwithstanding, the heart of his argument remained much the same: There is a good, faithful Christian America that has been brought to mortal peril by the actions and views of another part of the nation that is secular and immoral. Secular America was the problem, to which Christian America—and more specifically, that portion of Christian America that takes its direction from him, Robertson, and their fellow televangelists—was the solution.

And Pat Robertson? In the broadcast of September 13, he repeatedly endorsed his colleague's remarks (§§11, 13, 15) and he closed the interview by saying: "Jerry, this is so encouraging, and I thank God for your stand. We just love you and praise God for you. . . . And, thank you, my dear friend, for being with us" (§21). Four days later, on September 17, he issued a news release, saying he had been caught off guard by Reverend Falwell's remarks, which he characterized as "severe and harsh in tone." While he had "frankly, not fully understood" Falwell at first, he now found his dear friend's statements "totally inappropriate."[16]

IV

That Robertson did not understand what his guest was saying is among the very least plausible statements issuing from this episode. The kind of harangue Falwell delivered is a commonplace of the religious right, albeit usually offered in less public surroundings and less anguished times.[17] Much more credible is the defense Falwell mounted four separate times in his attempt at explanation.

> I sincerely regret that comments I made during a theological discussion on a Christian television program were taken out of their context. . . .

> I was . . . intending to speak to a Christian audience from a theological perspective about the need for national repentance.

> I was asking a Christian audience on a Christian TV program to claim II Chronicles 7:14 and repent.

> My mistake on the "700 Club" was doing this at the time I did it, on television, where a secular media and audience were also listening.[18]

Falwell thought he was addressing the faithful. Others, unschooled in the nuances of his discourse, might have mistaken his words for a mean-spirited, opportunistic rant directed against his political/cultural foes. The usual audience of the Christian Broadcasting Network, however, heard something different, something he expected them to find both familiar and welcome: a call for religious revival.

V

The highly significant term "revival" surfaced twice in Falwell's apology, where he described his performance as "sharing my burden for revival in America."[19] It was also a leitmotiv of the *700 Club* conversation, where Robertson eagerly asked his guest: "Do you think that this is going to be the trigger of revival, a real revival in the Church where we truly turn back to God with all our heart?"(§7). All of Falwell's subsequent remarks helped lay the groundwork for an affirmative answer, and from this perspective, his fulminations were preparatory exercises, not the heart of the matter. The interview's real climax came, rather, when he finally pronounced: "This could be, if we will fast and pray, this could be God's call to revival" (§16). This was the point toward which both men collaborated, trading well-honed licks back and forth like two experienced musicians.[20] Having reached their goal, Robertson moved things speedily toward closure, underscoring the desired conclusion.

> PAT ROBERTSON: Well, I believe it. And I think the people, the Bible says render [*sic*] your hearts and not your garments, and people begin to render their hearts and they weep before the Lord, and they really get serious with God, God will hear and answer. *We'll see revival.* I am thrilled to hear that about your church because it's happening all over. (§17; my emphasis)
> JERRY FALWELL: It's everywhere. (§18)
> PAT ROBERTSON: Yes. (§19)

VI

The theme of revival was already implicit in Robertson's opening salvos, where he harped on the familiar woes of abortion, pornography, and the prohibition on school prayer (§1). Concluding, "We have insulted God at the highest levels of our government" (§1), he argued that this was the reason why "God Almighty is lifting his protection from us. And once that protection is gone, we all are vulnerable. . . . And, the only thing that's going to sustain us is the umbrella power of the Almighty God" (§2). In these remarks Falwell—who was waiting offstage—seems to have heard a biblical allusion, if one can judge by his first words when brought on the show.

PAT ROBERTSON: Listen. What are you telling the church? You called your church together. What was your response at Thomas Road to this tragedy? (§5)

JERRY FALWELL: Well, as the world knows, the tragedy hit on Tuesday morning, and at 2:00 in the afternoon, we gathered 7,000 Liberty University students, faculty, local people together, and we used the verse that I heard you use a moment ago, Chronicles II, 7:14, that God wanted us to humble ourselves and seek his face. And there's not much we can do in the Church but what we're supposed to do, and that is pray. (§6)

Falwell cited this same passage, II Chronicles 7:14, in his explanations after the fact, where he reasserted the biblical basis for his views.[21] He has also cited it ceaselessly over the course of his career, although he is hardly unique in this, for it is a favorite of the religious right.[22] Famed as the verse to which Ronald Reagan opened his Bible at both inaugurations, also as the centerpiece of the "Washington for Jesus" rally (April 29, 1980) and the National Prayer Congress held in Dallas (October 26–29, 1976), events that many regard as founding moments of the New Christian Right, this passage is regularly made the touchstone of evangelical calls for personal and national revival.[23]

Understanding the significance of this verse begins with appreciating its position in the grand narrative of II Chronicles, which treats the history of Israel from Solomon to the loss of national independence. The book's fifth chapter tells how Solomon—richest, wisest, and most successful of Israel's kings—completed the temple, the grandest achievement in the nation's history. Chapter 6 continues, recounting Solomon's prayer of consecration, and at the beginning of chapter 7, God accepts the temple as his dwelling place on earth, filling it with his glory. Seven days of feasting and celebration follow, marking the high point of Israel's experience. There follows this passage:

> [11]Thus Solomon finished the house of the Lord and the king's house; all that Solomon had planned to do in the house of the Lord and in his own house he successfully accomplished. [12]Then the Lord appeared to Solomon in the night and said to him: "I have heard your prayer, and have chosen this place for myself as a house of sacrifice. [13]When I shut up the heavens so that there is no rain, or command the locust to devour the land, or send pestilence among my people, [14]*if my people who are called by my name humble themselves, and pray and seek my face, and turn from their wicked ways, then I will hear from heaven, and will forgive their sin and heal their land.*" (Revised Standard Version; my emphasis)

In II Chronicles 7:14—which answers a specific request in Solomon's prayer (6:26–27)—God anticipates future difficulties in his dealings with Israel but promises to play his part in reconciliatory processes that follow a regular, predictable sequence: (1) Israel sins and falls away from him; (2) He visits woes on his chosen, but fallible people, as a reminder and chastisement; (3) Israel repents, prays, and humbles itself; and (4) He restores their well-being. This is the scenario that Falwell, Robertson, and their regular listeners refer to as "revival," a process that can work at both a personal and collective level. Regularly, II Chronicles 7:14 is at the center of this discourse. Beyond the promise of this verse, however, there are other possibilities. As those who are steeped in the Bible know, God went on to speak more sternly to Solomon, making dire threats should sin and chastisement not be followed by repentance.

> [19]"But if you turn aside and forsake my statutes and my commandments which I have set before you, and go and serve other gods and worship them, [20]then I will pluck you up from the land which I have given you, and this house, which I have consecrated for my name, I will cast out of my sight, and will make it a proverb and a byword among all peoples. [21]And at this house, which is exalted, everyone passing by will be astonished, and say, 'Why has the Lord done thus to this land and to this house?' [22]Then they will say, 'Because they forsook the Lord the God of their fathers who brought them out of the land of Egypt, and laid hold on other gods, and worshipped them and served them; therefore he has brought all this evil upon them.'"

This passage, like the entire book of II Chronicles, was written well after the events to which it alludes and that it claims to prophesy. Those events include the quarrel between Solomon's sons, the schism of the kingdom into Israel and Judah, the conquest of Israel, scattering of the ten lost tribes, decadence in Judah, Babylonian conquest and captivity, and the final catastrophe: destruction of the temple. Later chapters of II Chronicles recount this sorry history as a narrative in which the religious and moral control the political, thematizing Israel's disasters as the consequence of unrepented sins and breaches of her covenant with God, not bad policy or military weakness.

After Solomon, things go downhill through a succession of kings, some better, but most decidedly worse, ending with Zedekiah, Solomon's antithetical foil. Of him, we are told: "He did what was evil in the sight of the Lord his God. He did not humble himself before Jeremiah the prophet, who spoke from the mouth of the Lord" (II Chron. 36:12). In subsequent verses

Zedekiah is shown to violate oaths, worship idols, subvert the priesthood, pollute the temple, and—most grievous of all—harden his heart against the Lord, refusing to repent (II Chron. 36:13–14). No repentance, no revival: whereupon, the final debacle.

> [15]The Lord, the God of their fathers, sent persistently to them by his messengers, because he had compassion on his people and on his dwelling place; [16]but they kept mocking the messengers of God, despising his words, and scoffing at his prophets, till the wrath of the Lord rose against his people, till there was no remedy. [17]Therefore he brought up against them the king of the Chaldeans, who slew their young men with the sword in the house of their sanctuary, and had no compassion on young man or virgin, old man or aged; he gave them all into his hand. [18]And all the vessels of the house of God, great and small, and the treasures of the house of the Lord, and the treasures of the king and of his princes, all these he brought to Babylon. [19]And they burned the house of God, and broke down the wall of Jerusalem, and burned all its palaces with fire, and destroyed all its precious vessels.

VII

Reflecting on II Chronicles during the Clinton years, leaders of the religious right found it easy to construct typological associations between the United States and ancient Israel, which they understood as the two privileged nations that enjoy(ed) a covenantal relation to God and a position of special favor. Pursuing this line of analysis, numerous items were brought into suggestive alignment, although rarely in quite so schematic or coherent a fashion as in table 3.1.

Had the attacks of September 11 come on Bill Clinton's watch, these comparisons could readily be extended. In such a construction, Clinton becomes Zedekiah; Osama bin Laden the new king of the Chaldeans "who slew their young men with the sword in the house of their sanctuary, and had no compassion" (II Chronicles 36:17), while the World Trade Center is conflated with the Temple: "And they burned the house of God, and broke down the wall of Jerusalem, and burned all its palaces with fire" (36:19). Disaster did not come with Clinton, however. Instead, God lifted his "veil of protection" some nine months after the inauguration of George W. Bush, whom Falwell and Robertson had vigorously supported.

VIII

The practical and hermeneutic problem the events of September 11 posed for the televangelists was how to read the attacks as a sign of God's wrath, while

	Israel	America
Golden Age	Solomon	"Founding Fathers" (an extremely vague period that sometimes seems to last from the New England Pilgrims through the Eisenhower years, 1953–60)
Age of Decline	Solomon's sons, schism of kingdom, sinful later kings, defeats by Babylon	*Engle v. Vitale* school prayer decision (1962), 1960s counterculture, *Roe v. Wade* abortion decision (1973), Carter "malaise" (1977–80), Clinton election (1992)
Prophets calling for repentance	Jeremiah et al.	Evangelists and televangelists
Disastrous last king, sinful and unrepentant	Zedekiah	Clinton? (esp. as revealed by Monica Lewinsky)
Outcome	Military defeat, national humiliation, destruction of the Temple	September 11: Only hope that disaster may be avoided lies in prayer and repentance

guarding against any inference that the new president—whom they had helped elect and whom they considered sympathetic to their views and agenda—was in any way responsible for America's loss of divine favor.[24] Not surprisingly, they avoided any comparison of that day's destruction to Israel's loss of the Temple. Rather than the final catastrophe, the attacks were a powerful wake-up call or—as Robertson hopefully put it—"the trigger of revival" (§7). Constituting President Bush as part of the solution, not the problem (no Zedekiah he!), they wanted him to be strengthened by the prayers of the faithful, so he could lead a repentant nation to revival and recovery of divine favor, followed by triumph and glory.

Under such a reading, the attackers of September 11 were not really the enemy in any absolute sense. As God's scourge, they were the instruments of divine purpose, sent to call the chosen people back from the brink. The real "enemy" occupied an ambiguous position inside the American nation, rather like that enjoyed by bin Laden's "hypocrites." They were those whom Falwell and Robertson denounced for having estranged America from the Lord and occasioned his chastisement. The preachers singled out the federal courts, (§§1, 12, 13), three organizations (American Civil Liberties Union, People for the American Way, National Organization for Women [§§10, 12, 14]), and numerous types of offender (materialists, hedonists, pornographers, abortionists, feminists, homosexuals, occultists, pagans, secularists, and Christ haters [§§1, 12, 14]). A pattern emerges from these lists, which recode Falwell and Robertson's enemies as a Fifth Column that flourishes inside America, putting the nation at terrible risk. Specifically, these two southern white males focus on persons, groups, and institutions that have challenged their preferred model of what family, society, and state ought to be, which is to say, patriarchal and Christian. Further, the Christianity they favor is of a decidedly maximalist sort, such that it ought to inform all personal choices and permeate all aspects of culture. Finally, and perhaps most important, their opponents include all who resist the assertion that the ideals these men champion are divinely ordained. As they understand themselves and their mission, it is to defend, restore, and maintain God's model of proper social and familial order against those who defy and threaten it.

Reading against the grain suggests, instead, that their goal is to stabilize the order they prefer and from which they benefit against all adversaries whose preferences diverge from their own. Rather than meeting the latter in principled debate and discussing, for instance, what advantages different means of family formation might conceivably have, they insist on the sacred (i.e., indisputable) status of their ideal, while denouncing all others as perverse and impious: an affront to God and (therefore) a mortal danger to the nation.

IX

We have mentioned the mild rebuke President Bush made in response to Falwell's tirade, which represented a bump, not a breach in their relations. While Bush—like his father and President Reagan before him—is not likely to deliver on most items of the religious right's agenda, he has need of this constituency, as does the Republican Party in general. Accordingly, he continues to court its leaders, albeit with discretion and delicacy, sometimes using symbolic gestures to do so. Gestures of this sort are often ambiguous and deeply coded, as we saw in the presidential address considered in chapter 2.

To be maximally effective for all concerned, they should (1) escape notice of those who might find them objectionable; (2) permit the president to deny them, should they attract any unwanted attention; and (3) be legible to the faithful as signs that their leaders are effective and enjoy a privileged relation to the president. Obviously, the leaders are free to exploit this last aspect, and they may also attempt to construe relatively innocent gestures as if they were signs of special favor.

Thus, as part of his response to September 11, Bush scheduled prayer ceremonies for September 14 at the National Cathedral, with Billy Graham as the featured speaker. Evangelicals and others saw in this a sign of his commitment to a program of revival, but Falwell made special use of this event. In his "Why I Said What I Said" statement of September 17, he inserted the following paragraph:

> On Friday, September 14th, President Bush invited me to join him, his family and administration and 3,000 others to the National Cathedral for a special Day of Prayer and Remembrance, where we asked God for His comfort, protection and wisdom.[25]

Whether or not Bush issued a personal invitation, Falwell strongly implied it was so, just as he tried to associate the presidential initiative with his theories concerning the "veil of protection" when he described the national ceremony as seeking not just God's comfort and wisdom, but more pointedly his protection. On September 20 Falwell released his "Why I Said What I Said" text once again, adding to it a new section entitled "We Must Pray for Our President." Here he came back to the prayer ceremonies of September 14 and wrote as follows, once again exaggerating the importance of his apparently rather limited participation: "I was honored to be present and to hear President Bush open his heart to the nation. He asked for our prayers." In the continuation of this new text, Falwell called on his followers to answer Bush's request and positioned himself as a leader in that endeavor. Awkwardly returning to his theme of prayer, repentance, and revival as the means to restore the "veil of protection," he concluded by saying, "God's children must not fail our Lord, our nation or our president. *Let us build a protective hedge about President Bush* and ceaselessly ask God to grant him the wisdom he will need for the awesome task ahead."[26]

In the weeks thereafter Falwell continued to work this theme, and in late October he gave it more formal status. In a missive released on October 22 and titled "Pray for America," he announced: "God has burdened my heart to

gather and galvanize 1 million prayer warriors to pray for America at this critical time in our nation's history." Discharging this sacred burden, he asked
people to visit his website (www.falwell.com) and promise to join "this
mighty prayer effort." In return, he would send them a flag lapel pin bearing
the slogan "Pray for America" and place their names on a list "which I will
present to President Bush in the near future." He directed the prayer warriors to focus their efforts on six recipients or objectives. First of these was
President Bush, along with Vice President Cheney, the cabinet, and Congress. After that came the military, those threatened by terrorists, the economy, and the families of those killed on September 11. Finally, the list re-
quested prayers "that God will bring revival to our land, beginning with His
church." To that end, II Chronicles 7:14 was cited, the only biblical passage
mentioned.[27]

The demands Falwell made of his recruits were not terribly onerous.
Those pressed for time could offer nothing more than a thirty-second prayer
while driving to work, so long as they did it each day. Those less encumbered
(or more highly motivated) could dedicate an hour out of each day to pray for
America. Whether God heard and answered those prayers is a question open
for discussion. Others, however, appear to have been listening.

Thus, in early January 2002 the *Chicago Tribune* reported that while President Bush was speaking to a group in California, he thanked all the American people who had prayed for him and his family. "People say 'Well, how do
you know?' I say 'Well, I can just feel it.' I can't describe it very well, but I feel
comforted by the prayer."[28] None of this made specific reference to Falwell
and his efforts, although he—like countless others—might think and claim
that his prayers were having an effect. Much more pointed were further
remarks, in which Bush used carefully chosen phrases to signal his endorse-
ment of major points in the televangelist's theology of revival and the argument he made on the *700 Club*.

> The prayer that I would like America to ask for is to pray for God's protection
> for our land and for our people. . . . [To pray] that there's a *shield of protection,*
> so that if the evil ones try to hit us again, that we've done everything we can,
> physically, and that there is *a spiritual shield that protects the country.*[29]

x

One could continue this story indefinitely, for there always are new chapters.
Although the interrelation of the religious and the political may seem aber-

rant under the constitutional doctrine mandating separation of church and state, it is hardly so within televangelical revivalism, where that doctrine is often explicitly rejected. Much more could be said here, but there is already a large literature that pursues these issues.[30] For the moment, by way of summary, let me simply assess this televangelical style of religion, making use of the four categories introduced in chapter 1.

Discourse.   Two different types can be identified: canonic Scripture and preaching. Although preaching is normally construed as a secondary elaboration of the primary truths enshrined in the Bible, things are more complex. The relation of these two discourses is better described as one of (un-acknowledged) mutual mediation, for the televangelists' situation in the present conditions the way they read, remember, cite, and interpret the Bible, while their knowledge of the Bible colors the way they perceive and engage their immediate circumstances. By minimizing their agency and masking their interests, while simultaneously insisting on the sacred status of the verses they cite, they attempt to claim the same sacred (i.e., authoritative and indisputable) status for the speech through which they advance their own favored views and projects.

Practice.   Here again, one can note several interrelated levels or types. First, there is a normative ethical order of practice that includes all actions enjoined or proscribed by preachers and the Bible, as they selectively cite and interpret it. Issues of sexual morality receive disproportionate attention, being the point where human desires most powerfully threaten to destabilize conventional family structures. Constituting such structures as divinely ordained, rather than historic accidents, cultural preferences, or the product of social negotiation, can thus be understood as an extraordinarily effective way to defend them against challenge and secure their perpetuation. (We will pursue this line of analysis further in chapter 4.)

A second order of practices includes those that are ritual in nature, including restorative actions like prayer, "revival," and atonement for ethical offenses and lapses. Finally, there is an order of practices reserved for the evangelists themselves, which involves the preaching of jeremiads (prophetic denunciations and calls for repentance in the manner of Jeremiah). Although these three orders are mutually supportive, a certain disjuncture can become apparent when the programs of self-humbling that preachers urge on others are contradicted by the arrogant, bullying behaviors they themselves evince, as happened so dramatically in Falwell's tirade of September 13.

Institution.   The directive apparatus of Protestantism centers on the office of the clergy but includes all organs that support and extend the latter: seminaries, churches, publishing houses, broadcast networks, Sunday schools, fund-raising drives, and so forth. By definition, the clergy is made up of people who, by virtue of special calling and/or training, claim the right to transmit God's word, as revealed in Scripture. Typically, American Protestant denominations have lacked a strong centralizing bureaucracy. As a consequence, clergy have tended to be entrepreneurial as they work to build their congregations, the size (and affluence) of which is a tangible index of their success.[31] Televangelism is the hypertrophic extension of such tendencies.

Community.   Given the difficulty of obtaining current statistics for the audience of noncommercial TV, it is hard to tell who was watching the *700 Club* when Jerry Falwell let fly. Figures from previous years suggest that perhaps 7 million people were tuned in, most of them white, female, southern or midwestern, rural, over fifty years old, and lower in income and education than the national norm. In all these respects, however, the audience for Pat Robertson's program is less extreme than that for religious television in general.[32] Somewhat easier than assessing the actual audience, but equally important, is the task of establishing who the televangelists believe they speak to and for. Close reading of their September 13 transcript reveals three different and interlocking social formations.

First is what Falwell and Robertson referred to as "the Church" and treat as their core constituency. Sometimes they used the definite article, as if for a monolithic entity (§§5, 6, 7, 8), and sometimes the plural, as if describing the local congregations that together constitute that monolith (§§1, 16, 20).[33] But in either case, they left no doubt that the church is the source of all that is good: the place where committed Christians assemble for prayer (§§6, 16, 20) and where spiritual regeneration occurs (§§7, 8, 16).

Second, there is the nation, usually referred to as "America" (§§2, 6, 7, 8, 12, 14, 16), but also as "the United States (§2), "our society" (§1), "our country" (§2), "the nation" (§14), "we" and "us" (§§1, 2, 6, 8, 12, 13).[34] Regularly, however, the televangelists' rhetoric divides the nation into two fractions. One, isomorphic with "the Church," is good, authentic, and holds the promise of redemption. The other, its antithesis, includes sexual dissidents and "all of them who have tried to secularize America" (§12). While indisputably part of the nation, the latter fraction poses mortal dangers to it, for such people have led America from its founding premises, estranged it from God, and caused him to lift his protection (§§10, 12).

Finally, there is the state, within which the televangelists recognize several interrelated lines of cleavage. Thus, they distinguish between local and federal government, with the issue of prayer in the schools as a prime site of conflict between them. Here local authorities and the good fraction of the American people (= the church) are thwarted by the Supreme Court, which—as on the issue of abortion—shows itself impious and tyrannical (§§1, 12, 13).[35] The judiciary is further contrasted to the executive, a site of hope when headed by a Christian, Republican president who welcomes the people's prayers (§6).

In other contexts the legislative branch comes in for criticism, and the televangelists frequently treat it as a microcosm where the nation's rival fractions do battle, conservatives versus liberals and Republicans versus Democrats. But in light of the much-publicized gesture that members of Congress made on September 12, Falwell chose to overlook their failings and internal lines of cleavage. On this occasion he represented all of Congress as his allies: proper, patriotic Americans and, as such, defenders of the church against the secularizers.

> Pat, did you notice yesterday? The ACLU, and all the Christ-haters, the People For the American Way, NOW, etc. were totally disregarded by the Democrats and the Republicans in both houses of Congress as they went out on the steps and called out on to God in prayer and sang "God Bless America" and said: "Let the ACLU be hanged!" (§14)

Mapping the way the televangelists conceive the relations among the constituent parts of the social (church, nation, state), one perceives a set of correlated binary oppositions, as shown in figure 3.1 below.

As should be clear from the preceding discussion, the televangelists' goal is not just to reconnect church and state or to modify the way First Amendment protections are commonly understood. Much more ambitiously, they hope to mobilize a religious community ("the Church") and rout the secularizers, whom they regard as a dangerous and inauthentic fraction of the nation. That accomplished, they would reconstruct the nation as a Christian

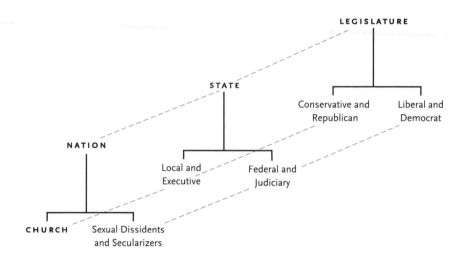

F I G U R E   3 . 1   Construction of the social, as implicit in the discourse of the Reverend Jerry Falwell and the Reverend Pat Robertson on the *700 Club*, September 13, 2001.

entity, for which a Christian state is the only appropriate political instrument and expression. State, church, and nation together can then enforce Christian ethics and promote a properly Christian culture. Less militant than al Qaeda, perhaps (given that the violence they employ in pursuit of their goals is rhetorical and not physical), the televangelists' religious ideal is equally maximalist, if Christian rather than Muslim.

CHAPTER FOUR

On the Relation of Religion and Culture

I

The category of "culture" has a built-in ambiguity, since it can refer both to a group or community (as when "my culture" = my people) and to some x that is a prime source of collective identity (as when "our culture" = our habits, customs, and so forth). Groups simultaneously define such an x and are defined by it in processes of mutual mediation, whereby each one is cause and effect (product and condition of possibility) for the other, much in the fashion of chickens and eggs. African American, Islamic, and Kwakiutl cultures, for instance, are constituted out of people who experience themselves as "African American," "Muslim," or "Kwakiutl" by participating in things they recognize as distinctive aspects and characteristic marks of their group. These may include seemingly superficial, but emotionally evocative signs such as wearing certain clothes, holding or moving one's body in a certain manner, and eating certain foods, either as part of one's regular practice or on ceremonial and public (i.e., highly marked) occasions.

Speaking a certain language (including dialect, subdialect, and local accent) is also important, particularly if we understand this to include sharing not just language per se, but a repertoire of stories, proverbs, jokes, and formulaic expressions, or even a textualized canon. One might extend the sense of "language" further still to include nonverbal systems of signification like art, architecture, dance, and music, or one might treat these as separate genres. But in either case, the extent to which one engages with local idioms and signifying practices conditions one's participation in culture. Also crucial are observance of a group's rituals, ceremonies, and etiquette, and—most broadly—manifesting behavior and showing a sensibility that those who constitute themselves as members of the group (1) recognize as their own; (2) recognize in themselves; (3) recognize in those people with whom—*as a result*—they feel bound by sentiments of affinity; and (4) recognize as lacking in those from whom—once more, *as a result*—they feel themselves estranged and constitute as Other.

Cultural identity and belonging are not simply ascribed or inherited by birth; they also—and more importantly—emerge from processes in which people are slowly educated by those around them to make judgments the group considers appropriate about a great host of things and to make meta-judgments about the relative value of their own and others' judgment. These judgments and metajudgments are made in many domains; to the extent that standards in these domains cohere and are shared by members of the group, we may speak of cultural integration.

Perfect integration, of course, is never accomplished, and there are always disagreements that separate fractions of the group from one another. These cultural divides indicate lines of actual or potential conflict, and they often correlate to differences that are socioeconomic, geographic, or doctrinal in nature. Such differences notwithstanding, a viable degree of integration remains possible even within a large and diverse population, so long as the group's defining principles are not overly narrow, rigid, or monolithic. Ideally they identify a range of possibility within which difference and discussion are permitted, even encouraged. As a result, actors can interact in situations of lively interest to debate specific judgments of given items, gradually renegotiating their values in the process, while also reaching finely tuned metajudgments about themselves and one another.

Those whose behavior and judgments consistently fall outside the range the group construes as normal (people whose clothes, food, or music strike others as weird and off-putting, for instance) thereby prompt metajudgments that identify them as outsiders: strangers in the fullest sense. Similarly, those whose judgments play at the edges of the culturally permissible are subject to metajudgments that relegate them to a correspondingly marginal social status. Marginality is the ordinary situation of children, for instance, whose failures of acculturation are tolerated and indulged precisely because they are understood to be temporary and corrigible (indeed, it is the task of child rearing to correct them).[1] More painful is the devalued status accorded those whose enduring deficiencies lead them to be branded philistines and bumpkins,[2] or those who once enjoyed full membership in the group, but having broken with its values, are judged to be deviant (e.g., criminals, heretics, apostates, traitors, or those Osama bin Laden refers to as "hypocrites"). "Culture" is thus the prime instrument through which groups mobilize themselves, construct their collective identity, and effect their solidarity by excluding those whom they identify as outsiders, while simultaneously establishing their own internal hierarchy, based on varying degrees of adherence to those values that define the group and its members.[3]

II

A second ambiguity that plagues the category of culture is the distinction between what sometimes gets called "high" culture or Culture with a capital *C*, as opposed to popular and mass culture, that is, culture in the minuscule. Both usages have some finite legitimacy, as well as their own internal problems, the one being more elitist and belletristic, the other more anthropological and democratic. If one seeks to relate them, however, the problem becomes identifying what this capital-*C* Culture is, specifying how it differs from its lowercase homophone, and assessing how the two interact. In the preceding discussion, we have focused almost entirely on lowercase-*c* culture, which can be understood as the sum of all communications circulating within a group that the group recognizes as distinctly its own and through which it differentiates itself from others. Culture with a capital *C* is a highly significant subset of this totality.

More precisely, capital-*C* Culture consists of the "choice" works and "select" genres that enjoy privileged status, social cachet, and official support. It is the subset of culture most valorized by the fraction of society that is most valorized, and that represents itself—with considerable, but never total success—as the custodian and arbiter of values for the group. Different social fractions can (and do) play this role in different societies and historic moments. Sometimes it is elders, particularly male elders, who are able to decide what really counts. Alternatively, this may be the prerogative of aristocrats, priests, intellectuals, the wealthy, or those who are able to convert their material and nonmaterial assets—the offices they hold and the respect they enjoy—into control over the institutions and processes with prime responsibility for cultural judgments and metajudgments.

Within the operant logic of such systems, it is claimed that the things-judged-best by the people-judged-best hold this status because they embody the ideals toward which all members of the group ought ideally to aspire, but that only truly "Cultured" or "cultivated" souls can fully appreciate and internalize.[4] If one steps outside that logic, however, and asks where these ideals come from and whom they benefit (a move far easier to make when considering a culture other than one's own), the self-serving aspects of the process become evident. Regularly one finds that a well-situated fraction claims as one of its privileges (and one that is key to preserving the others) the right to speak for the group as a whole. In this capacity, they misrepresent—occasionally in cynical fashion, but more often with sincere conviction—opinions that redound to their own benefit as if these were abstract and normative values. To use Gramscian terms, capital-*C* Culture is nothing other than hegemony, while lowercase-*c* culture is everything hegemony seeks to suppress, contain, and devalue.

III

In specifying the *x* that is the content of culture, I would begin with aesthetics and ethics, the domains in which groups articulate and enact their characteristic and defining preferences, or what some are inclined to call their "values."[5] Aesthetics includes all practice and discourse concerned with "taste," that is, the evaluation of sensory experience, including all matters of form and style. Ethics, on the other hand, concerns itself with "morality" in the form of abstract tenets, concrete practice, and casuistic evaluations regarding specific behaviors performed by (and upon) specific categories of person: How does a gentleman treat a lady? What can a beggar expect from a lord? Must one answer a psychopath truthfully? Can one kill in self-defense? For vengeance? For the good of the nation? On behalf of the faith?[6]

Every item of culture—every act of speech, piece of behavior, product of craftsmanship, and every human subject—offers itself, himself, or herself as an example of what is good (an ethical object) and/or what is pleasing (an aesthetic object). As such, it submits itself to members of the community for their evaluation. "How good is this image of the good?" it implicitly asks. "How pleasant is this experience of the pleasing?" To reach such judgments, those who are hailed as audience, market, or critic call into play everything they have retained from all the other items of culture they have encountered and all the judgments they have heard offered in the past. And as they do this, other members of the group observe and make metajudgments about them: "How good is this person's notion of the good?" becomes the question. "How pleasing is her appreciation of the pleasing?" Beneath which lie further questions: "How fully does she share and appreciate the values our group takes as its own and seeks to foster? Do her judgments conform sufficiently to those we share that we may safely regard her as one of us? Or do they show her to be marginal in ways that make us hold her at a distance and treat her with suspicion, even disdain?"

IV

Were ethics and aesthetics the sole components of culture, we might expect a good deal of volatility in the cultural—and social—order, as judgments of the good and the pleasing would constantly be revised in the course of incessant debate. As most of the world's populations over the full course of history attest, however, culture usually involves a third component that has a unique capacity to stabilize and buttress the others. This is religion, which invests specific human preferences with transcendent status by constituting them as revealed truths, ancestral traditions, divine commandments, and the like.

Thus, to cite an obvious example, groups everywhere establish specific principles of family formation, kinship structure, and property inheritance as defining bases of their social organization. These are all threatened, however, by the power of sexual desire that, in and of itself, has little concern for social norms, the construction of enduring affective relations, or the welfare of potential progeny. Societies can guard against the corrosive possibilities of untrammeled eros by making sexual relations a social, moral, and legal concern, but they can also go further still. The proposition "Thou shalt not commit adultery" (Exodus 20:14) gains its force not only from recoding "nonmarital sexual intercourse" (an aesthetic, i.e., sensuous pleasure) as "adultery" (an ethical offense), but also from four framing devices. Together, these constitute the prohibition not just as an item of common sense, civil law, or normative custom (human constructs all), but as a specifically religious injunction, whose authority derives from its infinitely more-than-human source. These frames include: (1) Placement of the injunction within a book constituted and recognized as sacred Scripture; (2) the prior narrative, which culminates in Exodus 19, where Moses receives revelation from God on Mount Sinai; (3) identification of Exodus 20 as God's direct discourse. "And God spoke all these words, saying . . . " (Exodus 20:1); and (4) the opening words of the discourse attributed to God, which remind its hearers of their historic relation to this deity, their dependence on him, and their obligation to do his bidding. "'I am the Lord your God, who brought you out of the land of Egypt, out of the house of bondage. You shall have no other gods before me'" (Exodus 20:2–3).

The shift from aesthetic or ethical to religious discourse effects a qualitative transformation of enormous importance. Human propositions, precepts, and preferences are (mis)represented as distinctly more than human, with the result that they are insulated against criticism by mere mortals. Direct challenge having been largely precluded, critics find space to maneuver within the interpretation of propositions now accorded transcendent status, as in the nuanced hermeneutics and ingenious casuistry of priests, theologians, and jurists. Space for more radical forms of contestation can also be found within the religious, although they have their dangers. Heresies, heterodoxies, folk beliefs and practices, calls for reform, claims of miracles and revelations, theological disputes, liturgical squabbles, anti-clerical jokes and gossip are all such moments of struggle.

Returning to the specific example introduced above, we should note that groups concerned with stabilizing "family values" need not limit themselves to (purportedly) divine prohibitions on sexual relations outside marriage. They can also attempt to preempt desire itself by placing restrictions on the appearance and comportment of its men and, more often, its women.[7] When justified on aesthetic or ethical grounds (concerns for style and good taste, on the one hand; modesty and propriety, on the other), attempts to de-eroticize dress and demeanor are open to disputation via arguments American parents find depressingly familiar ("That's so old-fashioned," "You treat me like a child," "None of my friends have that rule"). If religious discourse can recode the same restrictions as transcendent principles and divine commands, it can quash—or disarm—much of this resistance. A believing Muslim woman who covers her hair with a scarf, for instance, need not view this as a surrender to her parents' wish to keep her asexual, nor to patriarchal domination in general. Rather, she is encouraged to regard this as an act of self-fashioning, executed in conformity to precepts established by God, revealed through his prophet, and maintained by his people. The scarf helps constitute her not only as a moral subject, but as a part of the community whose faithful members preserve and are defined by this practice.

In the form of routinized practices mandated and supported by religious discourse, a community's characteristic preferences are experienced as sacred duties, not simply human choices.[8] For better and also for worse, the more thoroughly a community's preferences can be encompassed within the religious, the more stable that community becomes. Up to this point, we have tended to treat maximalism as the desire for religion to colonize all aspects of culture. Viewing things from an inverse perspective, we can now recognize that it also involves the desire for the other aspects of culture—specifically, a group's distinctive ethical and aesthetic preferences—to secure themselves by grounding themselves in religion.

v

Largely because of its unique capacity to stabilize vital human concerns by constituting them as transcendent, religion has been a central component of most cultures. Even in western Europe, the church was the central institution of society, chief source of collective identity, and final arbiter of truth until the Reformation and Wars of Religion fractured Christian unity in the sixteenth and seventeenth centuries. Even through that turbulent period, religious discourse continued to inform most human practices, leaving relatively little space for autonomous—that is, secular—ethics or aesthetics. Only with the Enlightenment did the possibility of such autonomy emerge, and this should be understood—as should the Enlightenment itself—as a reaction against the prior hegemonic position of religion in culture. That reaction, moreover, was prompted by disgust at the unprecedented violence of the Religious Wars, which threatened Europe with social, political, and cultural disintegration of unprecedented dimensions.

Voltaire spoke of the Wars of Religion as having unleashed "a type of barbarism that the Herulii, the Vandals, and the Huns never knew."[9] The critique of religion he advanced—along with other Enlightenment philosophes from Bayle, Locke, and Hobbes through Hume, Diderot, Helvétius, d'Holbach, Lessing, and others—is not incidental to or detachable from the bulk of their thought. Rather, they should be understood as having struggled to replace a well-established regime of truth with one of their own creation, whose methods, standards of expertise, problematics, authority structures, and institutional centers were still emergent. The older hegemon had "faith" and "revelation" as its epistemological watchwords, theology and doctrine as its prime discourses, orthodoxy and salvation as its goals, the church as its chief institution. Against this, the philosophes made "reason" their rallying slogan and "enlightenment" their goal, while polemically redescribing their adversaries' concerns as "idle superstition."[10]

Here it is worth recalling that publication of the *Encyclopédie* was (temporarily) suppressed by decree of Louis XV for its "irreparable damage to morality and religion," while Pope Clement XIII threatened those who read or owned it with excommunication.[11] Nor was the Pope wrong to feel threatened, for the project of the philosophes was a radical revision of culture that would displace religion from its dominant position, thereby freeing up ethical and aesthetic debate and reflection. This audacious endeavor was undertaken, moreover, in the wake of bloody religious conflicts demonstrating that religion is not of necessity a stabilizing force. For when rival aesthetic and ethical preferences are couched in religious terms, far from being suppressed, the conflict can be gravely exacerbated. For the rival parties now fight not only for their styles of dress, recreation, sexual or commercial morality, but for their faith, and with correspondingly increased ferocity and determination.[12]

Ultimately, it was Kant who brought the campaign launched by the Enlightenment to a compromise conclusion. The relation among his four major treatises reflects his attempt to restructure culture, and my own analysis reflects his categories. Thus, the *Critique of Practical Reason* (1788) and the *Critique of Judgment* (1790) treat ethical and aesthetic questions respectively, while the *Critique of Pure Reason* (1781; revised 1787) establishes philosophy as both necessary and sufficient for sound judgments in these two other domains. The three together form a triad of grand concerns—the Good, the Beautiful, and the True—sound knowledge of which is possible, but only through the exercise of philosophic reason. Philosophy thus assumes the controlling role in culture earlier played by religion, and Kant's fourth major work, *Religion within the Limits of Reason Alone* (1793), considers what to make of religion. There he develops the argument that religion is best suited to metaphysical questions like the existence of God and the immortality of the soul, where certainty is impossible, reason inadequate, and faith particularly appropriate. Religion is thus not overthrown altogether, but given a privileged, if marginal sphere of activity. Insofar as educated European elites were persuaded by these arguments, a new regime of truth took shape, which gave rise to a new type of culture.[13]

Among the prime beneficiaries of this structural transformation was the secular nation-state, which learned to derive its legitimacy from the people it governed rather than God, and which assumed responsibility for countless functions previously discharged by religious institutions: law, education, moral discipline and surveillance, social relief, record keeping, and others. The media of civil society—philosophy, literature, the arts, sciences, journalism, and popular culture—also gained at religion's expense, becoming prime venues in which ethical and aesthetic issues are seriously engaged and debated.[14] Commerce also gained enormously, for when aesthetics and ethics were no longer stabilized by religion, tastes could shift more freely and rapidly than ever before. It was this that made possible the appearance of fashion as an industry, novelty as a commodified desideratum, and a rapidly expanding capitalist economy predicated on the capacity to manufacture not just goods, but desires free to change, because recognized as strictly temporal.

VI

In subsequent centuries in those parts of the globe where the Enlightenment's influence has been most strongly felt, the place of religion in culture has shrunk to ever smaller times, spaces, and topics: Sunday morning church services, children's bedtime prayers, certain holidays and rites of passage. The transformation of Christmas from the high point of the liturgical year to the centerpiece of the shopping season is diagnostic. The trend has not been one of unremitting secularization, however, for there have been numerous reversals, revivals, and movements of principled opposition.[15] Most of these have been prompted by an acute sense of moral decline, particularly among those who feel that relaxed controls on sexual desire pose grave threats to marriage, the family, and what they are prone to call "everything that is decent." While one might dispute their phrasing, as well as their goals, this perception is not entirely wrong. Where Kant expected philosophical reason to stabilize ethics and aesthetics much as religion had previously done, it has proven inadequate to the task. Even more thoroughly marginalized than religion, its influence rarely penetrates beyond college classrooms and a few little-read publications.[16] Rather than philosophy, it is the market that has come to play the central role in modern (also postmodern) culture, and its influence is hardly stabilizing.

Although it is undoubtedly simplistic, as a heuristic device it is useful to distinguish two alternate models of culture. These are meant as Weberian ideal-types: logical poles, between which lies the more complex, variegated, and realistic middle ground in which most historic and social experience actually transpires. Having sounded that caveat, let me delineate the religiously maximalist form of culture that existed in all parts of the globe prior to the Enlightenment and contrast it with the minimalist form that was (par-

Maximalist	Minimalist
Religion = the central domain of culture, deeply involved in ethical and aesthetic practices constitutive of the community	Economy = the central domain of culture; religion restricted to private sphere and metaphysical concerns
Cultural preferences constituted largely as morality and stabilized by religion	Cultural preferences constituted largely as fashion and opened to market fluctuations
Religious authority secures coherent, ongoing order	Capitalist dynamism effects rapid expansion of wealth and power
Minimalist system experienced as powerful and intrusive; a serious temptation for would-be elites and a dangerous threat to all	Maximalist system experienced in two ways: a quaint, seductive diversion for some, and a resentful atavism, capable of reactionary counterattacks

tially and imperfectly) realized in some parts of the globe during the nineteenth and twentieth centuries.

VII

The adoption of the minimalist model had many consequences for Europe,
North America, and Japan. Chief among these were the expansion of economic wealth, state power, and industrial technology facilitated by dimin-
ished religious constraints on greed, violence, and scientific inquiry. Their
increasingly minimalist stance toward religion was hardly the sole factor
that enabled the Euramerican powers to colonize the rest of the world, but it
is hardly insignificant. And where they did establish control, liberal as well
as Marxist regimes attempted to disseminate minimalism as a—perhaps
the—constitutive feature of "modernity" and the necessary precondition for
"progress."

Later, in the period and process of decolonization, Europeans and Americans sought to transfer state power to postcolonial elites whom they had
trained and cultivated, inter alia, to internalize the minimalist ideal and
model. Only such people could be trusted to create a secular state, a robust
civil society and dynamic economy, and to protect these against the pressure
of other more "traditional" members of their society. Such people—who also
get termed "fundamentalists" or "fanatics" when their protests become too
strident—see these features of minimalism as exogenous residues of an
alien order. Whatever admiration they may have for the material prosperity
and technological accomplishments that accompany "modernization," "Wes-
ternization," or (as I would have it) "minimalism," they also raise principled
objections. Those whose aesthetic and ethical preferences are still stabilized
by religion regard a culture where this is no longer the case as debased, corrupt, driven by infantile desires of the pleasure principle, and unchecked by
any mature concerns, transcendent truths, or responsible authority.

This is the perspective of a Sayyid Qutb, Mohamed Atta, or Osama bin
Laden as they contemplate what Qutb came to call *jahiliyyah,* the barbaric
state of spiritual ignorance and rebellion against God's sovereignty. According to their analysis, Islam overcame *jahiliyyah* and is the only alternative to
it, which is why Islam must stand firm—even counterattack—against the
resurgent *jahiliyyah* that spreads from the infidel West.[17]

Although they struggle against an endogenous and not a foreign enemy,
the perspective of Pat Robertson, Jerry Falwell, and the American religious
right is similar in most other ways. With their calls for prayer in the schools,
evangelical revival, and a return to the Bible, they seek to reverse the Enlight-

enment's restructuring of culture. Their goal is to restore religion to the controlling position it enjoyed, for example, in Puritan New England, from which it can define communities and stabilize embattled hegemonies in ethics and aesthetics. Or as they put it, "restore traditional, God-given values."

Others are making similar attempts in other parts of the globe: governing parties in Iran, Israel, India, and the Sudan; powerful movements in Algeria, Afghanistan, Egypt, Turkey, parts of eastern Europe, central Asia, Pakistan, and Latin America. Sometimes they gain their immediate objectives, and sometimes they do not, but whatever success they have comes wrapped in cruel irony. Restoring religion to its dominant position within culture hardly puts an end to conflict; it simply ensures that a culture's most bruising conflicts will assume religious, rather than ethical or aesthetic character, and in that form they can be more destructive than ever. When one rejects the Enlightenment's values en masse and dispenses with its model of culture, one risks not just a return of the repressed, but novel Wars of Religion. Postmodern critiques have made us acutely aware of the many shortcomings associated with the regime of truth, style of culture, and practices of power introduced by the Age of Reason, and these are real enough. It is, however, worth remembering what the Enlightenment accomplished, which involves reading it in historic context and contrasting it with what came before, also with what could come after.

CHAPTER FIVE

Religious Conflict and the Postcolonial State

I

Although it is tempting to treat the September II attack as a unique and unprecedented event, it is also instructive to consider it alongside other conflicts since the 1970s that share certain features, particularly those where insurgent religious groups have challenged state elites. Most often this has occurred in postcolonial contexts where structural problems inherent to the nation-state have become exacerbated, specifically the potential for contradiction between nation and state.

While the conjunction of these two entities has become so ubiquitous as to seem natural, inevitable, and unproblematic, they can—and should—be kept analytically separate. Thus, the term "nation" designates a population that constructs and sustains a unitary collective identity.[1] "State" refers to a governmental apparatus that manages the political affairs of the nation(s) for which it takes responsibility and over which it exercises power. Although the idealized model of self-determination posits perfect congruence between the two, there are abundant examples of states that rule over multiple nations (the United Kingdom, with its English, Welsh, Scottish, and Irish populations; the former Yugoslavia, with its Slovenes, Croats, Bosnians, Serbs, Montenegrins, and Kosovars; more extreme still are the older imperial states of the Hapsburgs, Ottomans, Romanovs, or Qing, and sprawling conglomerates like Malaysia and Indonesia). Similarly, there are nations spread among multiple states, desperately seeking to establish one of their own (Kurds, Basques, Palestinians; Germans and Italians before unification; Poles in the periods of partition).

Although nation and state came together in the West during the nineteenth century to produce the distinctive sociopolitical formation of modernity, the two have separate genealogies and, as a result, somewhat divergent characters. Thus, the modern state is a child of the Enlightenment, born of reaction to the Wars of Religion. It was the carnage of the Thirty Years' War (1618–48) and the social turmoil of the English civil war (1642–53) that prompted Hobbes to write *Leviathan* (1651), the founding text of the modern state. There he described humanity as naturally disposed to a "War of all

against all" and envisioned a new, more powerful, specifically political apparatus as the sole means to check such destructive propensities.[2] To this end,
others subsequently pressed to build up the state by, inter alia, reducing its
dependency on religious institutions for ideological and bureaucratic functions (legitimation; education; definition, dissemination, and enforcement
of moral standards; record keeping; etc.).

The modern nation, in direct contrast, originated in Europe with attempts to expand capacities for organized violence by peoples who felt themselves menaced by more powerful neighboring states.[3] Its crucial moments
are (1) The *levée en masse* and revolutionary festivals (1792–94), through
which the Jacobins mobilized the French nation to defend itself against in-
vaders and enemies within;[4] (2) the response of early Romantics, Fichte
above all, to the Napoleonic wars (1806–13). Seeking to rally a defeated people, they emphasized common language, history, culture, soil, and "blood"
as potential sources of unity for an emergent "German nation" then still politically fragmented in many separate principalities;[5] and (3) the response of
the French to defeat in the Franco-Prussian War, German unification, and
the loss of Alsace-Lorraine (1870–71). These events produced the Third Republic, which organized massive efforts to cultivate patriotism, civic identity,
and national integration.[6]

Depending on circumstances, religion can provide a prime source of national identity (as in the case of Serbs, Israelis, or Pakistanis); connect insurgent groups with coreligionary supporters (Catholics in Northern Ireland,
Tamil Hindus in Sri Lanka, Palestinians); or define an internal cleavage that
needs to be overcome by stressing other sources of unity within the borders
of a pluralistic state (as in the case of Belgian, Nigerian, or American nation-
alisms). In any of these cases, moreover, the nation can acquire a quasi-
religious aura of its own, becoming the moral, spiritual, and ritual community that calls forth the highest devotion of its members, imbuing their lives
with meaning and purpose. The greatest work ever written in the sociology
of religions, Émile Durkheim's *Elementary Forms of the Religious Life* (1912),
is, at its core, a discussion of how nationalism becomes the chief religion of
a putatively secular, but only nontheist modernity.[7]

The picture I am trying to develop is that even in western Europe, where
the nation-state formation initially took shape, there is an unresolved tension between the secularizing character of the modern state and the potentially religious character of the nation. A second contradiction exists between
the state as an instrument designed to contain (or monopolize) violence and
the nation as one with the capacity to mobilize and unleash it. And when Eu-

rope exported the nation-state formation to the rest of the world via colonialism, further levels of complexity were added.

Most volatile of all is the situation created when Europeans bequeathed a state committed to the project of minimalizing the role of religion in culture to postcolonial elites. Having internalized Euramerican models and ideals as part of the self-fashioning that prepares them for power, such people may embrace a liberal understanding of "secularization" as a key element of modernity. That notwithstanding, they rule over and are accountable to largely religious nations. Having never suffered a trauma like the European Wars of Religion, the population in general see no need for minimalizing initiatives, which they experience as a Western imposition threatening to the stability, dignity, and integrity of their culture. (Traditional elites—patriarchs, tribal leaders, and, above all, priests—can be counted on to defend that culture, while also defending their privileged position in it.) Their trauma was colonialism itself, which threatened—and in postcolonial guise continues to threaten—not just profanation of what is holy, but profound destabilization of cultural patterns in which religion is inextricably interwoven, that is, the ethical and aesthetic preferences for which religious discourse, practice, and institutions provide crucial support.

Against this general background, I want to sketch four types of conflict that have become common in recent decades. In order that their differences may become clear, I will cite several examples of each type and offer a summary diagram that calls attention to three separate analytic-*cum*-chronological moments. Thus, prior to the outbreak of conflict proper, the relevant tensions, contradictions, and lines of cleavage are still contained within the nation-state of the status quo ante. Then, as a result of precipitating factors, which are so varied and locally contingent as to defy generalization, specific fractions of the preexisting nation commit themselves to a struggle against others and also, quite often, against the state. Finally, there is a moment when the outcome of that struggle—actual or desired—becomes apparent.

II

Even in nations where the population is relatively homogeneous with regard to its religious affiliations, states designed along the Enlightenment model still tend to define themselves as secular or minimalist: that is, officially neutral and benevolently disinterested in questions pertaining to religion. The initial appearance of homogeneity may be deceptive, however, since broad variation often exists regarding the nature and intensity of the religious commitments held by different fractions of the nation. Some of these accept and are pleased by state neutrality, while others are deeply offended, particularly as they find themselves and their specifically religious concerns excluded from state support and consideration.

In this situation certain clergy and laypeople may come to understand and portray themselves as the most—or indeed, the only—faithful adherents of the nation's traditional religion. Such actors find they can make effective use of religious language, symbols, and signs of identity to authorize mass struggles against the minimalism of the state. Initially, their goal may be limited to forcing revision of specific policies: abortion laws in the United States, Sabbath closings in Israel, the sexual content of movies or standards for women's dress in Pahlavi Iran, to cite some obvious examples. Confrontations of this sort can play out in many ways, but the Iranian example reveals the extent of their potential, even when the state in question is relatively powerful by all conventional measures.[8]

In dealing with the demands of aggrieved groups who claim to represent the religious nation, a secular state runs clear risks. Should its responses be —or be perceived as—dismissive, insulting, indecisive, inconsistent, provocative, heavy-handed, arrogant, patronizing, or unsatisfactory in countless other fashions, leaders of such groups may use this to telling advantage. Most traditions possess a large discursive repertoire that knowledgeable actors can deploy, in open or densely coded fashion, to identify their immediate campaign with a sacred and transcendent cause, while representing themselves as heroic defenders of the faith against demonic, infidel, or apostate opponents.

As such rhetoric finds and persuades its audience, the movement will grow and may succeed in seizing the terms of debate, forcing the state and others to adopt crucial items of their discourse. Beyond this, they may become able to face down repressive organs of the state, which are, after all, staffed by people who share their religious identity and convictions, at least in nominal fashion. A crucial moment may come when rank-and-file soldiers have to decide whether to obey orders to fire on crowds. At issue is the question of whether their ties of affinity to those who identify themselves with the (religious) nation are more compelling than the demands of loyalty and obedience to their superiors, who defend the (secular) state. Should they decide not to shoot, as happened during the Iranian Revolution, other changes will rapidly follow.

As insurgents meet with success and gain hope of winning the struggle, their goals may well expand from the desire to reform select policies to that of seizing power and reconstructing the state along explicitly, even rigor-

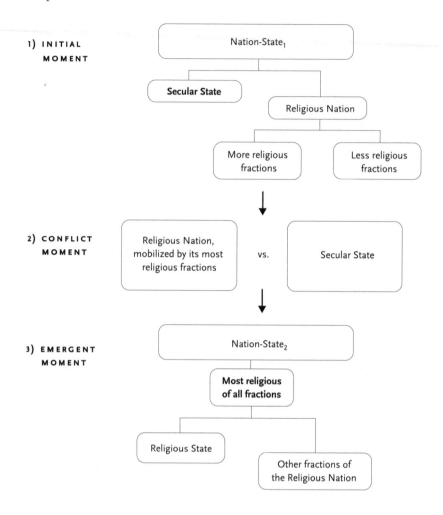

1) **INITIAL MOMENT**

Nation-State₁

Secular State

Religious Nation

More religious fractions

Less religious fractions

2) **CONFLICT MOMENT**

Religious Nation, mobilized by its most religious fractions

vs.

Secular State

3) **EMERGENT MOMENT**

Nation-State₂

Most religious of all fractions

Religious State

Other fractions of the Religious Nation

FIGURE 5.1 Religious reconstruction of the state. Power relations among the various entities are marked by primacy along left-right and up-down axes. The dominant entity is also marked by boldface type.

ously, religious lines. Examples other than the Islamic revolution in Iran include the activity of the Muslim Brotherhood in Egypt and Algeria, the Taliban in Afghanistan, various religious parties (who frequently change names as a result of repression) in Turkey, Orthodox activists in Israel, Hamas in Palestine, the religious right in the United States, and—to cite a more historic example—the crusade waged by Falangists, Carlists, and Cedistas in the Spanish civil war (see fig. 5.1).⁹

III

Somewhat different is the situation of a secular state and a religiously pluralist nation, for here an important part of the state's ideological justification is
the claim that it alone is capable of maintaining peace among the religious
groups within its borders, while exercising even-handed power over them.
This is the model developed in Europe during the Enlightenment and designed to preclude the internecine slaughter of the Wars of Religion. Beyond
its local utility, it also had advantages when European powers extended their
colonial reach into Africa and Asia during the eighteenth and nineteenth
centuries, since it permitted them to aggregate local populations of widely
different religions and cultures within a single colony. Here the new over-
lords could maintain control of "the natives" by playing one fraction off
against another, all the while claiming that their presence was necessary to
protect vulnerable minorities against their more numerous, bloodthirsty, or
"savage" neighbors.

As Europeans withdrew from their overseas empires, they bequeathed
this model of the secular (or religiously minimalist) state to those among
their former colonial subjects whom they most trusted to maintain it in this
form, having cultivated them for this purpose. Whatever its benefits—and
they are not negligible—the secular state remains inconsistent with precolo-
nial traditions, and insofar as it bestows state power on the most successfully
Westernized fractions of the population, it has created numerous difficulties. Of particular interest is the situation that develops when members of
the majority religion in postcolonial nations feel that the state operates to
their systematic disadvantage, while benefiting members of minority religions: people from whom they may also feel estranged on other grounds. In
such circumstances the disaffected can find powerful instruments of agitation and mobilization in narratives that recall the grandeur of "their" nation
in the past. That nation, as they tell it, was constituted primarily, if not exclusively, by their coreligionists, and their interests were protected by a state
whose power and very existence were sacralized by its mission of supporting
"their" religion. In such narratives—as much mythic as historic—they do
not just celebrate a past now gone. Rather, they deploy that past as critique of
an objectionable present; also, as a means to imagine and help realize the future of their desire.

By way of example, one could cite the situation of Sinhala Buddhists in Sri
Lanka and that of Muslims in the Sudan.[10] The best example, however, is India, where a large fraction of the Hindu population, made up of those whose
caste, education, and income let them expect neither important positions

within the state nor substantial largesse from it, has embraced a militant Hindu nationalism, as initially championed by two pressure groups, the Rashtriya Swayamsevak Sangh (RSS) and the Vishwa Hindu Parishad (VHP), later adopted by the Bharatiya Janata Party (BJP). Attempting to mobilize a Hindu voting majority, which otherwise is subject to fracture along lines of caste, the BJP employs a rhetoric that dwells on past Hindu glories (mythical and historical), thematizes Muslims as eternal enemies (not members!) of the Indian nation, and charges that Muslims and other minorities retain unfair preferences and advantages introduced by the English in the colonial era. The activist groups also pursue more militant campaigns including, most dramatically, that which led to the 1992 destruction of the Babri Masjid Mosque in Ayodhya, a sixteenth-century structure that stood on a spot that activists have insisted is the birthplace of the Hindu god Rama. Although this spectacular act of demolition prompted weeks of rioting and more than three thousand fatalities (the worst communal violence since the 1947 partition), the BJP rode the wave of religio-nationalist sentiment to victory in the 1996 national elections. Other parties, however, were committed to the constitutional construct of a secular state and refused to join in a parliamentary coalition, with the result that the BJP fell within two weeks without having formed a government. Learning from the experience, the BJP again won a large electoral majority in 1999 and pledged it would refrain from erecting a temple to Rama on the disputed site, whereupon it was able to assemble a governing coalition. The construction of such a temple remains a prize project of the RSS and VHP, however, who use this demand to exert pressure on "their" government to embrace a more religious and less secular understanding of the state. The situation remains volatile, and sparked new violence in February and March 2002 (fig. 5.2).[11]

IV

The third case begins more or less where the second leaves off: that is, with a situation in which the dominant religious fraction of a pluralist nation enjoys systemic advantages vis-à-vis all others, including effective, if not necessarily unmediated or total, control over the state. In such instances the state may or may not be defined as religious, but even when nominally secular, it is anything but even-handed. Particularly complicated are colonial situations like that of Northern Ireland (and before 1921, of Ireland as a whole), where state power is in the hands of foreigners who favor the local fraction with whom they have religious affinity.

When the unequal distribution of advantages from the state—jobs and

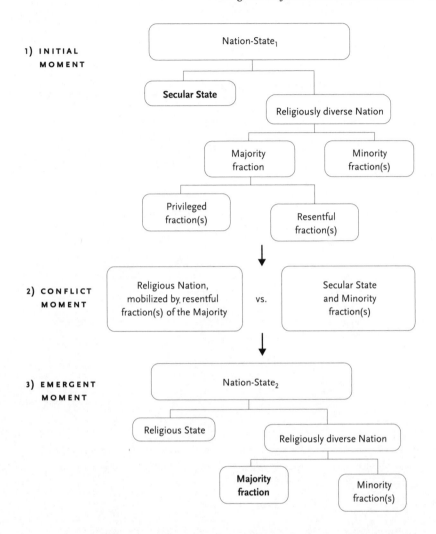

FIGURE 5.2 Construction of a religious hegemony. Power relations among the various entities are marked by primacy along left-right and up-down axes. The dominant entity is also marked by boldface type.

funds, for example, but also such things as simple respect and protection under law—is chronic and grievous, or perceived to be so, those communities who suffer can mobilize around their religious identity to challenge those of other faiths and the state that prefers them. Independence is usually their goal, as in the case of the Palestinian *intifada* against Israel, the struggle of

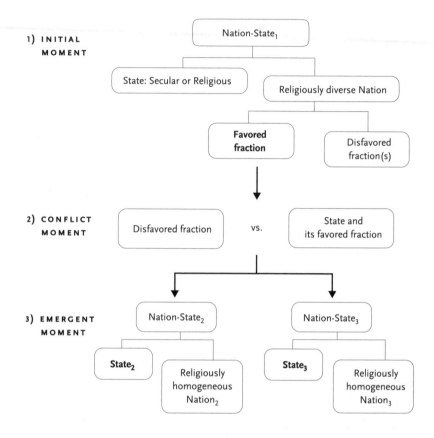

1) **INITIAL MOMENT**

Nation-State₁

State: Secular or Religious

Religiously diverse Nation

Favored fraction

Disfavored fraction(s)

2) **CONFLICT MOMENT**

Disfavored fraction vs. State and its favored fraction

3) **EMERGENT MOMENT**

Nation-State₂

State₂

Religiously homogeneous Nation₂

Nation-State₃

State₃

Religiously homogeneous Nation₃

FIGURE 5.3 Schism. Power relations among the various entities are marked by primacy along left-right and up-down axes. The dominant entity is also marked by boldface type.

Tamil Hindus against Sinhalese Buddhists in Sri Lanka, and that of Tibetan Buddhists against China. Alternatively, insurgents may pursue union with a nation-state controlled by their coreligionists, a strategy that worked for the Muslim minority of Cyprus and is favored by Catholics in Northern Ireland. In all of these cases, the issue of whether the new state is religious need not arise, so long as it can be expected to support the religious nation constituted by the insurgents (fig. 5.3).

v

Finally, there is the situation in which a modern nation-state deconstructs in decidedly postmodern fashion. At such times groups that were encompassed in the decaying formation may take advantage of the state's (temporary?) weakness to reassert other sorts of identity. Should leadership fall to their most militant fractions—as is likely to happen—they may also wage open war against once and future rivals, the state included. Sometimes the groups, causes, and communities to which people commit themselves on such occasions have little connection to issues of religion, as in the case of Somalia, Liberia, Rwanda, Burundi, and Bangladesh, where lines of kinship, ethnicity, patronage, language, and geography define the lines of cleavage. But religion can also play a role of decisive importance, as was true in the partitions of India and Palestine at the end of colonial rule, and in the Lebanese civil war of the 1970s and 1980s.

Elsewhere, religious considerations may be one of several correlated bases for the construction of communal identities, insofar as they replicate ethnic and linguistic lines of division. Thus, the battle among Bosnians, Croats, and Serbs was simultaneously one among Muslims, Catholics, and Orthodox, just as those that pitted Serbs against Kosovars and Macedonians against Albanians were simultaneously struggles between Orthodox and Muslims.[12] In the Caucasus, Muslim Chechens try to bring in their coreligionists in other regions (Ingushetia, e.g.) to fight the Russian state, which is as ethnically and religiously alien to them in its present as it was in its previous incarnations. And only a few years back, Christian Armenians fought Muslim Azerbaijanis. There is a chaotic turbulence to all these conflicts, where contending parties struggle awkwardly toward multiple goals. These include putting an end to an old, constraining state; constructing a new one of a different sort and along different lines; constructing (or reconstructing) a coherent and more or less homogeneous nation; extricating themselves from lingering connections to other emergent nations, from whom they feel bitterly estranged, but who were recently fellow citizens (or dominated subjects) of the same state; winning international recognition, financial and diplomatic support; and gaining whatever territory possible at their enemies' expense.

Such cases are not limited to postcommunist environments, and one can imagine scenarios in which Nigeria could come apart (as it almost did during the Biafran civil war of 1967–70), or the Canadian state could give way to new nations constituted by francophone Catholics, anglophone Protestants, and indigenous peoples. Indonesia and the Philippines present still more complex meltdown possibilities. Still, it is probably no accident that the most spectacularly destructive situations should arise in the former Yugoslavia and the former Soviet Union. Here disparate nationalities were dominated

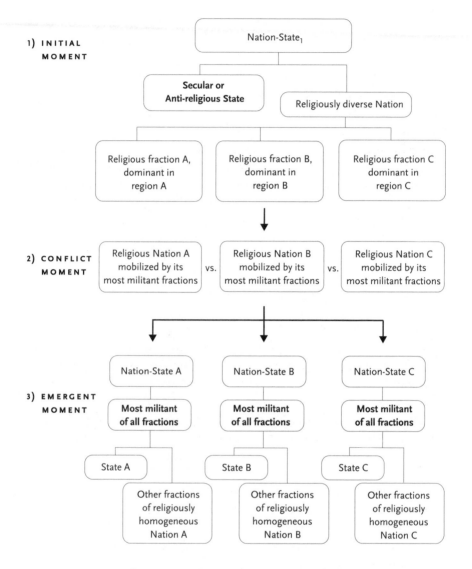

FIGURE 5.4 Devolution. Power relations among the various entities are marked by primacy along left-right and up-down axes. The dominant entity is also marked by boldface type.

by atheist states unconstrained by the Enlightenment model of minimalism and even-handedness in matters of religion. Rather, state elites here undertook the more radical project of suppressing religious ideology and institutions to the best of their ability. With the inevitable reassertion of the repressed, religion became a favored site of resistance to the state and a privileged instrument for the rallying of nationalist sentiment. Reactions of this sort are apparent in Poland, Afghanistan, and Tibet, and in historical uprisings against earlier anti-clerical regimes, as in the case of the Cristero movement in the Mexican Revolution, the Vendée rising in France, or the Carlist wars in nineteenth-century Spain (fig. 5.4).

VI

Confronted with the disquieting reality of religious conflict, popular wisdom typically comforts itself with the ironist's refrain: "How sad to see wars in the name of religion, when all religions preach peace." However well intentioned such sentiments may be, they manage to ignore the fact that all religions sanction, even enjoin the use of violence under certain circumstances, the definitions of which have proven conveniently elastic. In similar fashion, academic commentators often regard the religious side of conflicts like those in Sri Lanka or Northern Ireland as relatively unimportant, or, alternatively, they deplore it as a debasement of all that is properly religious. Although one can empathize with those who offer such views, their analyses rest on an understanding of what constitutes religion that is simultaneously idealized and impoverished. While theological considerations may play a relatively small part in distinguishing the rival communities, those communities quite emphatically define—and experience—their collective identity in terms of religion. Those who periodically observe that the Northern Ireland Troubles, for example, "have nothing to do with religion" are misled by a definition of religion that unduly privileges belief and discourse. This ignores the other aspects of religion treated in chapters 1 and 4, particularly the way communities differentiate themselves from others by distinctive practices, symbolic markers, and cultural preferences (aesthetic and ethical), all of which have their religious dimensions. The colors one wears, the names one gives one's children, and one's participation in or resistance to parades of the "Marching Season" all connect one to paradigmatic moments of the past and signal one's fidelity to either the Protestant or Catholic cause. These ritual gestures evoke mythic moments and effect membership in explicitly religious communities in much more powerful ways than does espousal of a specific doctrine or creed.[13] A joke I was told in Belfast in 1999 is apposite:

73

> A group of lads encountered a stranger standing outside their pub. The man looked a bit peculiar, since he wore saffron robes, had a shaven head and a curious tranquillity about him. Unable to make much of the fellow, one of the lads approached him. "Good evening," he said. "Is it a Catholic or a Protestant you're being?" Upon hearing he was a Buddhist, the lad paused a moment, then continued, "I see. Is it a Catholic or a Protestant sort of Buddhist you're being?"

For the sake of definitional clarity, I regard conflict as the situation that arises when rival interests can no longer be contained by the structures and processes ordinarily competent to do so. As a result, after an indeterminate period of confusion and crisis, normal competition moves into phases that are more open, bitter, confrontational, costly, and, frequently, violent. Like all others, communities and institutions that define themselves in terms of religion still wage their conflicts primarily around rival claims to scarce resources: people, territory, wealth, positions of power, and economic advantage, but also such nonmaterial resources as dignity, prestige, and all manner of symbolic capital. Unlike other groups, however, they are concerned to reconcile the gritty nature of their struggles with the elevated precepts featured in their discourse. That those charged with this difficult task may accomplish it only via a selective reading of the relevant texts and tradition or ingeniously strained hermeneutics does not normally detract from the enthusiasm with which their results are received.

Those results permit would-be combatants to define themselves and their cause as not just moral, but holy: chosen people, sacred land, divinely ordained offices, inviolable ancestral traditions.[14] At the same time, they can define their adversaries in terms of religious alterity of the Manichaean sort employed by President George W. Bush and Osama bin Laden that we considered in chapter 2. In so doing, they constitute the foe as debased, benighted, even demonic: "infidels," "pagans," "heretics," "apostates," "Great Satan," and that splendid tautology of cold war rhetoric, "godless atheist Communism." Such understandings condition the morale, intensity, and commitment of those who adopt them, and they have the potential to transform even the most sordid squabbles into *jihads* and crusades, from which retreat, surrender, and compromise are equally inconceivable.

The Western modern nation-state was created, in large measure, as a check against the violence and destruction unleashed in religious conflicts of this sort. From the eighteenth century until the late 1970s, it was quite successful in this task, if not in that of suppressing conflict more broadly. During this period, wars between nation-states replaced wars between religious communities as the largest and most common form of conflict, as the state sought to constitute itself—in Lenin's phrase—as a monopoly on the legitimate use of force.

In recent decades contradictions between nation and state have manifested themselves with particular force in postcolonial settings, where the nation-state form is exogenous in origin and antithetical to local traditions concerning the relation of religion and culture. Had this intrusive institution delivered on its promise to provide material well-being for its citizens, conceivably it might have been embraced with enthusiasm. In many places, however, it has served chiefly to enrich and empower members of a state elite who are identified with and dependent on former colonial powers but largely alienated from the populations over which they rule. Under such circumstances, dissatisfaction is natural enough and can take many forms. Sometimes dissidents seek change in policies or state personnel. At other times they struggle to redefine the principles on which the state is constituted and the way it relates to the nation. The Islamic Republic of Iran, the Taliban regime in Afghanistan, the institution of *Shari'a* law in northern Nigeria, and President Bush's "faith-based initiative" are all experiments of this last type, none without its problems.

The al Qaeda network represents something else again, insofar as its aspirations point beyond the struggle to reconfigure extant states along more religious lines. Rather than being a militant fragment within a nation-state, it understands and constructs itself as simultaneously the militant vanguard and the most faithful fragment of an international religious community. The goal it articulates is the restoration of Islam in a maximalist form and its consequent triumph over its internal and foreign enemies. Those enemies include, first, the Western powers, who are not only non-Muslims, but non-, even anti-religious ("infidels"); second, postcolonial state elites, whose Islamic commitments have been egregiously compromised ("hypocrites"); third, that part of the Enlightenment project committed to religious minimalism and ascendancy of the secular state.

Seen from a Western perspective, this seems a quixotic project, atavistically hearkening back to our Middle Ages, when the church, not the empire, was society's central institution.[15] At the same time, there is something decidedly postmodern about it. Like multinational corporations, global communications conglomerates, and transcontinental Mafias of other sorts, al Qaeda recruits and trains its personnel, raises and circulates its funds, selects its targets for operations, and pursues its goals all without particular regard for international borders, national identities, and questions of state sovereignty. It poses a threat not only to the United States and western Europe, but also to the governments of Saudi Arabia, Pakistan, Egypt, and others.[16] Most broadly, however, it challenges the Enlightenment restructuring of culture and its preferred model of the nation-state, which entails a secular state, pluralistic nation, and minimalist religion. Indeed, it can be seen as an attempt to invent the institutions that will displace state and nation alike in a still emergent future.

CHAPTER SIX

Religion, Rebellion, Revolution

I

Over the course of the last century and a half, countless theories of the nature of religion have been advanced, and most—deservedly—have fallen into oblivion. Many of these theories present religion as a *Ding an sich,* a system of pure ideas utterly divorced from any social, political, or historic context, and while some of these remain influential, they will not concern us here.[1] Of those that remain, I would suggest that most can be grouped in two broad classes, which for the sake of convenience I will label the "romantic" and the "materialist" positions, and which for all their differences prove to be paradoxically similar in the last analysis.

For their part, the "romantic" theorists have sought to show the multiple ways in which religious discourses, institutions, and practices (including myth, theology, and cosmology as subcategories of discourse, and ethics and ritual as subcategories of practice) serve the maintenance of society in a positive fashion. Thus, they have pointed to the ways in which religion effects social integration; charters central institutions and patterns of organization; provides a coherent set of ethical values and behavioral norms; furnishes a sense of meaning, purpose, and worth; and sustains hope in the face of suffering and death. Included within this "romantic" grouping would be such theoreticians as those of the école sociologique, the functionalist school of social anthropology, and the Chicago school of history of religions.[2]

In contrast to the "romantic" emphasis on the services rendered society as a whole, "materialist" analysis has tended to argue that religion serves only the interests of certain privileged strata, preserving their wealth, power, and position, while actively inhibiting any threats to them. This is accomplished in a number of ways, most notably by casting the material interests of the privileged or dominant into ideological form and presenting these as eternal truths; rechanneling the discontent of subalterns into otherworldly aspirations; and, where conflict is inevitable, canalizing it into ritual forms where it can be purged and rendered harmless. Within the "materialist" position, I would group Marx (although not necessarily Engels or certain other

Marxists, including Benjamin and Gramsci), the Manchester school of social anthropology, and such French semiologists as Roland Barthes.[3]

For all their differences—and I have no intention of minimizing them—the "romantic" and "materialist" views are nevertheless in close agreement in many ways. Essentially, both perceive religion as fulfilling the same function: providing solace for the suffering and stability for society. Where they differ is on the value they accord this function.

There are problems with such formulations, however, and these have come to light as scholars turned their attention to what Vittorio Lanternari termed the "religions of the oppressed."[4] Among these have been grouped such movements as the African Independent Churches, the Native American Ghost Dance, and the Cargo Cults of Melanesia, wherein religion provided an effective rallying point for opposition to the imposed religion, ideology, and values of colonial powers, and in some cases to colonial rule itself. Nor are such movements confined to the colonial situation. Better understanding of Third World millenarianism, chiefly as the result of the work of such scholars as Wilhelm Mühlmann, Peter Worsley, and Kenelm Burridge,[5] stimulated reexamination of numerous episodes within the history of western Europe, including such messianic, millenarian, and heretical movements as the Italian Lazzarettisti, the medieval Taborites and Pastoureaux, and the followers of Sabbatai Sevi, as assessed by such scholars as E. J. Hobsbawm, Norman Cohn, Bernard Töpfer, and Gerschon Scholem.[6] Even the major revolutionary upheavals of modern Europe came in for reexamination, as the religious content of the English civil war and the French Revolution were assessed by Christopher Hill, Michael Walzer, Christopher Dawson, Michel Vovelle, and others.[7] In none of these instances will a simple view of religion as "solace for the suffering and stability for society" suffice. Consideration of data from the long history of millenarian rebellion in China, such groups as the Kharijites, Mahdists, Nizaris (Assassins), Wahhabis, and the Muslim Brotherhood within Islam, or the Iranian Revolution of 1977–79 only serves to buttress this conclusion.[8]

For all that I am not ready to dispense entirely with the view advanced by "romantic" and "materialist" theoreticians alike. It is not so much an inaccurate view as it is an inadequate one, its inadequacy lying in the fact that it is insufficiently dialectic, for it attempts to reduce religion to a single, monolithic entity, whereas even in the politically and technologically simplest societies, multiple religious forms, styles, contents, currents of opinion, and organizational structures are always present.

Following Marx and Gluckman, society should be seen as a field of tension in which a variety of fractions compete for limited resources of wealth, power, and prestige. But pace the former, one cannot legitimately conclude that religion and ideology are the tools of one fraction only, the ruling class, a point George Rudé has forcefully made of late.[9] In the remarks that follow, I hope I can suggest a more subtle and flexible view of things, one that permits us to assess how different religious forms attend the needs of different fractions within society at different moments in their struggle.

II

The chief division within the social field of tensions is that between the dominant class or fraction and all others, the dominant being that which controls the bulk of wealth and prestige, along with the means of production; occupies most positions of institutional authority or effectively controls those who do occupy such positions; and holds a monopoly on the legitimate use of coercive force.

Invariably, the dominant fraction disseminates a characteristic ideology through all segments of society, propounding a set of fundamental values and principles that, while expressed in terms of lofty abstraction or eternal truth, nevertheless serves to further the interests of those who hold power. Most often this ideology is couched in religious or para-religious forms.[10] It is this ideology and the institutional means for its propagation that I would call the "religion of the status quo." Whatever other tenets may be included in such a religion, I would expect to find present a legitimation of the dominant fraction's right to hold wealth, power, and prestige; an endowment of the social order with a sacral aura, mythic charter, or other transcendent justification; and a valorization of suffering within this world, concomitant with the extended promise of nonmaterial compensations for such suffering.

Religious institutions are established and professionals recruited for the propagation of this religion throughout society, and being vitally interested in the success of such propagation, the dominant fraction supports these institutions and individuals in any number of ways. Often they are granted a monopoly in receiving and/or administering education. Beyond that, the religion of the status quo may be established as a state church, membership and attendance being required of all citizens. Again a secure and often sizable income can be granted to its institutions and professionals through such mechanisms as state salaries, tax exemptions, forced tithes, and grants of property.

A secure income is indispensable, for the labor of religious professionals is not itself directly productive. Occasional claims to the contrary notwithstanding, one cannot create bread by prayers and sacrifices. As a result, priests must rely on the support of others, either those whose labor is directly productive or those who have control of excess wealth. To the extent that religious institutions must support not only the basic subsistence requirements of its personnel, but also expensive edifices, trappings, ritual displays, and the like, it is driven to rely more and more on the support of the dominant social fraction. One should stress, however, that such a relation is not parasitic in the strict sense, for the religion of the status quo tenders valuable service to the dominant fraction by propagating its ideology in return for such support, although such a bald quid pro quo is rarely explicit.[11]

The role of Confucianism in traditional Chinese society provides an excellent example of the religion of the status quo.[12] Within that society four broad classes are recognized: literati, peasants, artisans, and merchants, ranked in that descending order. The crucial division within this quadripartite system, however, is between the literati—who are called "great men" (*chün-tzu*), hold all official positions, are the only educated members of the populace, and engage in mental labor alone, directing the work of others—and members of all other classes, who are called "small men" (*hsiao-jen*) and engage in physical labor to produce goods and services. Literati were the largest landowners, in addition to which they were exempt from taxation, conscription, the *corvée*, arrest without imperial approval, and corporal punishment. By virtue of explicit sumptuary laws, they were entitled to different styles of dress, food, and goods from the other classes. Although admission to literatus status was theoretically open by means of examination, it was only members of literatus families who could obtain the education necessary to pass.

Throughout the history of China, from the Han dynasty (206 B.C.–A.D. 220) onward, the official religion of the class of literati was Confucian. Central to their doctrine was an insistence upon the ancestral cult and filial obligation as the proper model for all social relations, all other dealings being seen as permutations of the father/son bond: ruler/ruled, superior/subordinate, "great man"/"small man." The central ethical values encouraged were thus, in the words of Etienne Balázs, "respect, humility, docility, obedience, submission, and subordination to elders and betters."[13] An elaborate system of ritualized practice (*li*) was adopted, continuously studied and refined, and propagated among all strata, the purpose of such rituals being, as T'ung-tsu Ch'ü put it, "to make social distinctions clear and to regulate men's desires according to their statuses."[14] One final element in the Confucian system is the well-known doctrine of the "Mandate of Heaven," whereby any given emperor is said to be selected by heaven itself. His legitimacy thus derives from the sacred realm, not from the populace, and sacrifice to heaven was always an imperial monopoly.[15]

For all its differences of detail, the system bears strong resemblances to the Church of England under James I and Charles I, to choose a convenient example.[16] There, by virtue of the patronage system, parish parsons were regularly appointed by the local landed gentry and thereafter represented their interests and those of the king. Universities existed primarily for the training of clergy, admission being largely reserved for younger sons of wealthy families, to whom conservative values came easily and were further reinforced in the course of their training. Clergymen were crucial to the dissemination of information and formation of opinion through their preaching, for membership in the state church and attendance at services were mandatory, while censorship of all printing and licensing of all teachers were in the hands of church bishops. Among the most important of the doctrines propagated were those of sin and hell whereby those who suffer were taught that this suffering was the just result of their own sinfulness remediable only through the church's absolution and the grace of Christ. Also prominent was the divine right of kings, with its corollary view of the state as the sovereign's body politic, he being society's head and other citizens the lesser members of its body, in descending order according to their position within the social hierarchy.[17] Sir John Eliot (1592–1632) succinctly and dispassionately articulated the purpose of such doctrines and institutions, observing, "Religion it is that keeps the subject in obedience."[18] Here, as in China, we see a religious ideology that serves the interests of the dominant social fraction, and a religious institution supported accordingly by that dominant fraction.

Thus far, however, as examples of the religion of the status quo I have mentioned only instances in which members of the dominant fraction belong to the same broad sociopolitical entity as do the other members of society, which is to say, noncolonial situations. But we must also ask whether a similar "religion of the status quo" exists within a colonized state, our focus of study being in this case colonial missions. This constitutes an extremely important, but a very difficult question for a number of reasons, not least of which is the lack of reliable data and serious study. Mission reports tend to be self-glorifying, and objective scholarship has rarely gone beyond expressions of understandable distaste to assess seriously how missions operate and what ideologies they propound.[19]

We can, however, venture a few broad and provisional generalizations, noting first of all the strong support given to missions by colonial administrations, which regularly cede control of education and medical service to them, coerce colonial peoples to attend them, and provide them with abundant free colonial labor. The ideology propagated by missions is a selective Christianity consciously adapted for colonial consumption, which regularly insists that salvation can be won only through faith in the Christian god as revealed in the Bible and explicated by missionaries. Colonial expansion is thus cast as an altruistic crusade, bringing hope of salvation to those otherwise irrevocably lost. To avail themselves of that hope, however, colonized peoples must first acknowledge the superior knowledge and authority of Europeans and adopt the beliefs and practices they prescribe, abandoning traditional ones wherever necessary. Salvation is thus presented as an exclusive club, admission to which is European-controlled, non-Europeans being accepted only insofar as they become appropriately reformed and submissive. Again we see an ideology that serves the interests of the dominant fraction, spread by an institution that the dominant fraction supports, and this symbiosis I take to be the hallmark of the religion of the status quo.

We must also note that the characteristic goal of the religion of the status quo is ideological hegemony throughout the state or empire in which it is active, and to this end it energetically proselytizes, attempting to disseminate its contents to all segments of society. Full hegemony, however, lies always beyond its grasp, and it meets strong resistance among various sectors of the population, particularly those which have most reason to be dissatisfied with the givens of the status quo and are most alienated from the dominant fraction. In most—but not necessarily all—instances, these are elements of a colonized population or the lower socioeconomic strata, which is to say those who have the least interest in preserving social stability and whose sufferings are too great for the solace extended by the religion of the status quo.[20]

Within such groups there regularly exist or come into being religious ideologies quite different from that propagated by the religion of the status quo, together with institutional structures for their preservation. Such ideologies and institutions—which I would term "religions of resistance"—result from the inevitable failure of the religion of the status quo to permeate and persuade all segments of society. The extent to which they flourish at any given time thus provides an inverse index of the ideological hegemony of the dominant fraction and its religious apologists. As a rule—although it is hard to generalize—such groups do not themselves proselytize widely beyond the geographical locus and social milieu in which they are rooted, their first goal being not so much hegemony as mere survival, to which end they create cohesive, defensible, insular communities.

Whereas there will as a rule be only one religion of the status quo within a given society at any given time, the variety of religions of resistance that may thrive simultaneously is well-nigh endless, and history attests to a rich variety of exemplars. They may be ascetic, libertarian, or orgiastic; impassioned, cathartic, or quietistic; utopian or nihilist; esoteric, mystical; militant or pacifist; authoritarian, egalitarian, or anarchist; and so on ad infinitum. No attempt to reduce them to a small number of "ideal-types" is possible without serious distortion. As a class, they are best characterized by a negative feature: their refusal to accept the religion of the status quo in part or in toto. And however innocuous the doctrines or activities of such groups may seem, this refusal constitutes at the very least an implicit threat to the interests of the dominant fraction—a threat that is regularly answered by their stigmatization or suppression.[21]

The most obvious religions of resistance are those movements that have been labeled "heterodox" by religions of the status quo: Buddhists and Taoists in China; Jains and Buddhists in India; Huguenots, Lollards, Hussites, Anabaptists, and countless "heretic" groups throughout European history, not to mention Jews and Freemasons; Baha'is and Isma'ilis in Iran; and Shi'ites in Arab nations, to name but a few. Beyond these, one must also include the numerous independent churches and spirit possession cults of Africa; most of the Melanesian Cargo Cults in their early phases; the Peyote and Sun Dance religions of North America, as well as all surviving traces of traditional Amerindian religions; such Afro-American movements as Candomblé, Umbanda, Santería, Shango, Vodun, and Ras Tafari; not to mention the rich variety of black churches, Pentecostal groups, and new religions in the United States.[22]

Notwithstanding their diversity, all of these groups, and countless others as well, share a common feature: their resistance to a religion of the status quo. In the first place, all religions of resistance espouse a set of values that differs in some measure from that of the religion of the status quo. Thus, for instance, the Taoist ideal of *wu-wei*—"non-action, harmonious acceptance of the natural Way (Tao)"—stands in marked and self-conscious contrast to the Confucian attempt to regulate all social dealings.[23] Again, the Isma'ili vision of what Islam (and, a fortiori, society) should be—mystic, revelatory, passionate—is vigorously opposed to the legalism and rationality of Sunni doctrine.[24] Yet again, the ideal of Indian collectivism advanced within the Sun Dance confronts and undercuts both the competitive Protestant-ethic individualism fostered by white society and the hedonic individualism prevalent on many reservations, as argued by Joseph Jorgensen in his masterful study of the Sun Dance.[25]

Different values, taken seriously, result in different modes of action, and the religions of resistance can be seen to encourage practices at some degree of deviance from those encouraged by the religion of the status quo. This may result in a more rigidly disciplinarian or ascetic ethical stance, as with the Puritans or such Islamic reformers as the Wahhabiya and Sanusiya, or in a more latitudinarian position verging even upon antinomianism, as with the Brotherhood of the Free Spirit or the "Seven Sages of the Bamboo Grove" during the later Han dynasty.[26] The specifics are of little theoretical consequence. What matters most is that such deviance implies—better yet, enacts—defiance.

While the membership of religions of resistance tends to come from the lower strata (including colonial populations within that description), their leadership as a rule does not. Rather, leaders tend to be members of the "marginal intelligentsia," to use Jean Baechler's phrase.[27] Working from Chinese data, Yuji Muramatsu showed how the leaders of popular religious movements consistently came from what he termed a "middle stratum" of monks, sorcerers, out-of-work priests, fortune-tellers, and degree holders who had failed to win a place within the official bureaucracy, all of whom thus fell between the literati and the peasant class. Such individuals, themselves discontent and in need of support, introduced new discourses to lower-class circles, articulating and giving focus to peasant discontent, while winning adherents and a secure income for themselves in the process.[28] Within colonial situations the picture is quite similar, with the added complication that it is usually either members of the traditional elite displaced by colonial rule or those members of the indigenous population who have traveled and gained experience of European ways who constitute the "middle stratum" that emerges to lead religions of resistance.[29]

Leaders of such movements are often termed "charismatic," in line with Weber's theories or simply through sloppy parlance, but as Peter Worsley has convincingly argued, this must be rejected as an inadequate description of a much more complex state of affairs. "Charisma," properly understood, is not so much a gift of individual personality as it is the following called forth by one who is able to catalyze latent discontents and extend the hope of overcoming them. Moreover, lacking the traditional indications of legitimate authority—titles, training, ordination, trappings of office, and so forth—

"charismatic" leaders regularly have recourse to an altogether different and superior source of legitimacy: the sacred itself, claiming that their authority rests on revelations or visions, direct experience of transcendent reality.[30]

Rituals that promote group solidarity form an important part of most religions of resistance, including such forms as initiations, oaths, communal meals, and the like. They may range from such spectacular displays as the Sun Dance or spirit possession séances to the seventeenth-century Quaker insistence on addressing all individuals as "Thou," a formalized pattern of practice that simultaneously stressed Quaker unity, differentiated them from all other members of society, and directly challenged the etiquette of social stratification and submission.[31]

Ritual healing is also a common feature of a great many religions of resistance. Its prominence is quite understandable given the clear needs of populations lacking wealth, power, and access to professional medical care; the prevalence of stress-induced illness among lower social strata; and the strong bonds that may be forged between healer, healed, and the family of the patient. More important than any of these, however, may be a point made by Michael Adas; within such religious movements, healing must also be understood metaphorically, the patients being simultaneously victims and representations of society itself.[32]

In terms of values, ethics, membership, leadership, and rituals, then, religions of resistance stand apart from religions of the status quo. In general, they much more closely resemble the "religions of revolution" that we will shortly consider. But here again there are instructive contrasts. For while a religion of resistance may ultimately become a religion of revolution, crucial differences separate the two. Religions of resistance define themselves in opposition to the religion of the status quo, defending against the ideological domination of the latter. Religions of revolution, on the other hand, define themselves in opposition to the dominant social fraction itself, not its religious arm alone, promoting direct action against the dominant fraction's material control of society. The Kikuyu Independent Churches, for instance, provide a good example of religions of resistance, their chief goal having been the preservation of traditional ritual forms, particularly women's initiatory rites, against missionary attacks.[33] In contrast, the Mau Mau were a religion of revolution, since they confronted British rule in general rather than just the missions, took an aggressive rather than a purely defensive stance, and focused on the issue of land, which, while it had profoundly religious dimensions (land being a major part of the Kikuyu ancestral cult), also represented the very means of production in Kenya for British and Kikuyu alike.[34]

In order for a religion of resistance to transform itself into a religion of revolution, it seems to me that three things must normally transpire:

1. Objective conditions within society (e.g., fiscal, economic, political, medical, nutritional, military, etc.) must worsen.

2. The religion of resistance must successfully articulate a new theory of political legitimacy, which denies the right of the dominant fraction to occupy its privileged position and the right of the religion of the status quo to dictate normative values.

3. The religion of resistance must overcome its insularity and begin to recruit actively, incorporating new adherents from segments of society previously absent from its membership.

Of these three, the first is undoubtedly the most important. Revolutions never result from religious factors alone, these being only ancillary to many other variables. When objective conditions are good—peace prevails, prosperity is general, and all segments of society are generally healthy and well fed—the task of the religion of the status quo is easily accomplished, and there is little opportunity for religions of resistance to mount a serious threat.

As conditions deteriorate, however, the task of the religion of the status quo becomes ever more difficult, at the same time becoming ever more vital to the continued rule of the dominant fraction. As suffering mounts, more spiritual balm must be applied, and as discontent rises, there is ever more need for its canalization into harmless outlets. Ultimately, the religion of the status quo becomes engaged in a desperate attempt to shore up a faltering regime, as when the Convocation of the Church of England, following the dissolution of the Short Parliament in 1640 and on the eve of civil war, instructed clergymen to preach the divine right of kings throughout the land.[35] That Charles's rule could not be saved by such means is now obvious but ought not prevent us from perceiving a more general point: in situations of true crisis, the task of the religion of the status quo is impossible, while every successful revolution results in part from the failure of the religion of the status quo to fulfill its regular function.

If declining objective conditions present grave problems to the religion of the status quo, conversely they offer rich opportunities to religions of resistance, which become more militant in their ideology, more strident in their rhetoric, and more active throughout society at large during times of hardship and crisis. In particular, groups with a strong eschatological or millenarian doctrine are apt to thrive, for they present a coherent and, to many, a satisfying picture of current ills, not just as aspects of social, political, or economic dysfunction, but as the birth pangs of a new age.[36] The prevalence of eschatological mythology within movements of social protest, moreover, is not accidental, but the direct result of the temporal structure of such myths, in which the world of the present is condemned as decadent or senescent, while a radically different mode of being is expected in the immediate future in the wake of an apocalyptic struggle.[37]

Millennial expectations alone, however, do not lead inevitably to revolution, as history abundantly documents. So long as the religion of the status quo is able to persuade the bulk of society that those who hold power do so with perfect legitimacy, even in a crisis situation they will be difficult to dislodge. The theory of divine right shored up many sagging monarchies for centuries, and it was only when the alternative theories of Hobbes, Locke, and Rousseau had become influential that the English, American, and French revolutions became possible.[38] While some would see in this the replacement of a religious theory of legitimacy with a secular theory, it is important to note that such was not the view of the chief actors to these revolutions, who saw such doctrines as the rights of man, popular sovereignty, and the social contract as no less sacred—in fact, much more so—than the divine right of kings. For the vast majority of them, the struggle was not one of secular ideology against religion, but of true religion against superstition.[39] One looks in vain for total nonbelievers in the French and English revolutions.[40] As Robespierre, the most fascinating figure of the French Revolution, put it: "It is not enough to have overturned the throne; our concern is to erect upon its remains holy Equality and the sacred Rights of man."[41] Nor is his religious language either accident or hyperbole, for it was the Jacobins, led by Robespierre, who sought to establish the cult of the Supreme Being in place of Christianity, and who referred to their messengers as apostles going forth to establish a new religion. In the words of Christopher Dawson, they "were not satisfied with political reforms or republican institutions. They dreamt of a spiritual republic based on moral foundations."[42] Lacking such a moral foundation, the ancien régime was rejected as illegitimate, its pretensions notwithstanding; legitimate authority, argued the Jacobins, derived from eternal reason and virtue alone.

The issue of legitimacy also lies behind the Nizari (Assassin) revolt against Sunni orthodoxy and the Seljuq Empire in the eleventh to thirteenth centuries, masked behind a theological and epistemological dispute. Whereas the Sunnis argued that learned speculation and reflection could lead to recognition of the truth in matters of law and religion, the Nizaris—like other Isma'ilis—insisted that this was not possible, and only the Imam, the legitimate descent of Muhammad through his daughter Fatimah and son-in-law 'Ali, could perceive and communicate the true esoteric meaning of the Quran.[43] Since certain Nizari leaders claimed to harbor or even be the hidden Imam, this was tantamount to claiming sole legitimate authority within the world. These issues were clearly posed during the siege of Isfahan in 1107, where Seljuq forces attempted to recapture the city from the Nizaris. Ahmad bin Attash, seeing his military position untenable, sought peace, and sent a message to the Seljuq sultan that his people were good Muslims who differed with their Sunni brothers only on their view of the Imam, a matter insufficient for conflict between them. In return, the sultan asked, "If your Imam were to permit you what the Holy Law (*Shari'a*) forbids and forbid you what it permits, would you obey him?" Receiving an affirmative response, the sultan continued the siege, ultimately slaughtered the garrison, and flayed Ahmad bin Attash alive, carrying his head in triumph to Baghdad.[44] Such severity becomes comprehensible when we recognize that the Nizaris had established a religion of revolution by framing a direct challenge to the theory of legitimacy propagated by the religion of the status quo.

But alternative theories alone, however cogent or persuasive they may be, are not in themselves sufficient for the formation of a revolutionary movement from a religion of resistance. Given their insular, defensive orientation and organization, such movements ordinarily do not possess sufficient numbers, expanse, or material wherewithal to pose a serious threat to the continued rule of the dominant fraction. It is only when religions of resistance are able to break out of their insularity, absorb other groups like themselves, and attract new members from other sectors of society that they can move toward revolution, and this the Nizaris had also done by uniting numerous centers of heterodoxy throughout Iran and Syria. Rather than remaining an island of resistance in their fortress of Alamut, they systematically spread their doctrines to other cities where a significant portion of the populace was disaffected with Seljuq rule and Sunni orthodoxy, inciting them to seize their cities and use them as bases for agitation, infiltration, and terrorism against other cities yet. Other movements have similarly progressed from a stage of resistance to one of revolution, often quite rapidly, as for instance, the Native American Ghost Dance, Kenyan Mau Mau, or Sanusiya of Cyrenaica during the Italo-Sanusi wars.[45] To cite another example, in her study of the Eight Trigrams Rebellion (1813), Susan Naquin has meticulously demonstrated how the eschatologically oriented Chinese sects collectively referred to as the "White Lotus Society" normally existed as small-scale, scattered devotional groups in times of relative prosperity, coalescing into large and powerful revolutionary movements in times of hardship and imperial decay.[46]

It is not enough merely to recruit new members, however, for a religion of revolution—and in addition to those I have mentioned, I would include under this heading such groups as the Yellow Turbans, Taipings, Kharijites, Mahdists, Maccabees, the Maori Pai Marire movement, the Maji Maji rebels of German East Africa, and also the Puritan coalition of the English civil war and the Jacobin coalition of the French Revolution[47]—must also forge a new bond of solidarity and common commitment among those who have been recruited. Although there are numerous means toward this end, one of the more important is ritual. Regrettably, a serious examination of the rituals employed by the religions of revolution lies far beyond the scope of this chapter, and I will thus only mention in passing the tremendous importance of the Ghost Dance, the Mau Mau oaths, or such massive ritual celebrations as Muharram 1978–79 in Iran or the Feast of the Federation and Feast of Reason in the early years of the French Revolution, before passing to the most extreme form of revolutionary rituals, which E. E. Evans-Pritchard, writing in another context, dubbed "rituals of collective obscenity."[48]

Deliberate sacrilege, sexual abandon, and wholesale violation of taboos appear frequently in moments of revolutionary upheaval, as has often been observed. As early as 1925, Pitirim A. Sorokin devoted a section of his *Sociology of Revolution* to "Perversion of Religious, Moral, Esthetic, and Other Acquired Forms of Conduct."[49] While more insightful and sensitive analyses have been offered by Roger Bastide, who saw in such phenomena a radical break with the past, and Kenelm Burridge, who spoke of them as a dialectic phase of "no rules," necessary before "new rules" can replace the old.[50] Occasionally conscious reeducation is evident, as in the public desecrations of the de-Christianizing campaign of 1793–94 in which asses dressed as bishops dragged the Gospels through the streets.[51] But in all such acts—and one could number among them the drink of blood with which the followers of Teng Mou-ch'i began their rebellion in 1442, the exhumation of the bodies of nineteen nuns by Barcelona crowds in July 1936, and many others[52]—another element predominates. Such spectacular gestures irrevocably bind those who have witnessed or participated in them together in an enterprise from which there can be no turning back. As Danton said to the future Louis XVIII, à propos of the Terror: "It was my will that the whole youth of Paris should arrive at the front covered with blood which would guarantee their fidelity. I wished to put a river of blood between them and the enemy."[53]

To speak of such actions as the Terror of the French Revolution as ritual is not to deny the reality of their effects. All human action is both symbolic and technical, that is, it simultaneously communicates something and accomplishes something. Within a revolution it is often hard to judge just which of these dimensions predominates, for the entire history of any revolutionary struggle—demonstrations, agitation, debate, battles, purges, and the like—can be interpreted as a series of iconoclastic rituals intended to dismantle the symbolic and ideological constructs by which the dominant fraction of the past sought to perpetuate its rule.[54] One of the clearest examples is regicide, which is not just the execution of a king, however much it is that, but the ceremonial destruction of the ideology of kingship.[55] During the trial of Charles I, Cromwell observed to Algernon Sidney: "I tell you, we will cut off his head with the crown on it."[56] When such actions are successful, they destroy both the ideology and the material power of the old dominant fraction. When unsuccessful, they are condemned as atrocities.[57]

Ironically, victory and defeat alike spell the end of a religion of revolution. Its rising defeated, it falls back to become a religion of resistance again, or disappears completely. Successful, it becomes a new religion of the status quo in the service of that fraction that it helped bring to power. Numerous changes come over its ideology and structure. Leadership is regularized, as, for instance, when the successful rebel Huang Ch'ao abandoned his former title, "Great Heaven-storming General," in favor of the title "Great Heaven-appointed General."[58] The material benefits available to a religion of the status quo are also assumed. Radical elements—particularly those retaining a strong eschatological orientation, antinomian tendencies, or extreme states of emotional excitation—are suppressed, often ruthlessly, as with Cromwell's treatment of Levellers, Ranters, Diggers, and Fifth Monarchists, or the desertion and proscription of White Lotus and Manichaean elements by Chu Yüan-chang after he had founded the Ming dynasty with their support.[59] The new disposition of wealth, power, and position that emerges from the revolution is now accorded legitimation, and the former religion of revolution sets about propagating its creed throughout society. What remains of its revolutionary thrust are some superficial trappings: a new set of festivals, system of nomenclature, or hagiographic corpus made up of martyrs to the cause.[60] The story of the revolution attains the status of cosmogonic myth, and deviations from the official version are branded heterodox or "counter-revolutionary."

As for the defeated religion of the status quo, it too assumes new form as a religion of resistance, albeit a very special one, which I would term the "religion of the counterrevolution." Its marks are profound nostalgia, condemnation of the new order as usurpers, and—in its early years, at least—active attempts to restore the dominant fraction with which it fell, attempts that can prove successful, as in the case of the Spanish civil war.[61]

III

At present it is easy to overvalue the role of religion within sociopolitical revolutionary upheavals, given recent events in Iran, Latin America, Ireland, Lebanon, and Poland, just as in the past it was easy to dismiss its role as relatively unimportant, or to ignore it altogether. Both tendencies strike me as unfortunate, and I prefer the view espoused by Georges Balandier, among others, of revolution as a total social phenomenon that embraces not only political, economic, and military issues, but artistic, cultural, and religious ones as well.[62] To ignore any of these areas—not to mention so apparently minor a point as changes in etiquette or fashion—is to impoverish our analysis accordingly.[63]

In accessing the religious dimensions of revolutionary phenomena, one must insist that religious movements and ideologies take multiple forms, and that no movement or ideology is frozen into a single sociopolitical stance for eternity. Rather, they are part of a dynamic process, shifting their orientation as the result of external events and their confrontation with other movements and ideologies rooted in different segments of society, representing different interests.

I have tried to suggest some of the complexities that attend the roles religion may play in any revolutionary situation. The categories I have proposed—religions of the status quo, religions of resistance, religions of revolution, and religions of the counterrevolution—are admittedly crude, and only begin to approximate the infinite and subtle range of possible variations. But such groupings are a step beyond the formulations of the "romantic" and "materialist" theoreticians with which we began, wherein religion was seen as a monolithic entity invariably championing the interests of stability, social integration, and the status quo.

In such a view, however, these theorists are not alone, for it is the very view propagated by the religions of the status quo themselves, something they voice most fervently when under attack from religions of revolution. Thus, for instance, immediately after the suppression of the Eight Trigrams Rebellion, the emperor Chia-ch'ing proclaimed that beyond the Confucian social and moral principles, "no so-called religion exists, and outside the principles of nature and the laws of the ruler, happiness may not be sought after; happiness proceeds from complying with orthodoxy, and misfortune from following heresy."[64]

As scholars, we are not bound to accept such formulations. That we have done so in the past, in some measure at least, is only the gauge of how powerful is such propaganda.

Final Instructions to the Hijackers of September 11, Found in the Luggage of Mohamed Atta and Two Other Copies

§1 In the name of God, the most merciful, the most compassionate. . . . In the name of God, of myself and of my family. . . . I pray to you God to forgive me from all my sins, to allow me to glorify you in every possible way.

§2 Remember the battle of the prophet . . . against the infidels, as he went on building the Islamic state.

THE LAST NIGHT

§3 Making an oath to die and renew your intentions. Shave excess hair from the body and wear cologne. Shower.

§4 Make sure you know all aspects of the plan well, and expect the response, or a reaction, from the enemy.

§5 Read al-Tawba and Anfal [suras 8 and 9, traditional war chapters from the Quran] and reflect on their meanings and remember all of the things God has promised for the martyrs.

§6 Remind your soul to listen and obey [all divine orders] and remember that you will face decisive situations that might prevent you from 100 per cent obedience, so tame your soul, purify it, convince it, make it understand, and incite it. God said: "Obey God and His Messenger, and do not fight amongst yourselves or else you will fail. And be patient, for God is with the patient."[1]

§7 Pray during the night and be persistent in asking God to give you victory, control and conquest, and that He may make your task easier and not expose us.

§8 Remember God frequently, and the best way to do it is to read the Holy Qur'an, according to all scholars, as far as I know. It is enough for us that it [the Quran] is the words of the Creator of the Earth and the plants, the One that you will meet [on Judgment Day].

§9 Purify your soul from all unclean things. Completely forget something called "this world" [or "this life"]. The time for play is over and the serious time is upon us. How much time have we wasted in our lives? Shouldn't we take advantage of these last hours to offer good deeds and obedience?

§10 You should feel complete tranquility, because the time between you and your marriage [in heaven] is very short. Afterwards begins the happy life, where God is satisfied with you, and eternal bliss "in the company of the prophets, the companions, the martyrs and the good people, who are all good company."² Ask God for his mercy and be optimistic, because [the Prophet], peace be upon him, used to prefer optimism in all his affairs.

§11 Keep in mind that, if you fall into hardship, how will you act and how will you remain steadfast and remember that you will return to God and remember that anything that happens to you could never be avoided, and what did not happen to you could never have happened to you. This test from Almighty God is to raise your level [levels of heaven] and erase your sins. And be sure that it is a matter of moments, which will then pass, God willing, so blessed are those who win the great reward of God. Almighty God said: "Did you think you could go to heaven before God knows whom amongst you have fought for Him and are patient?"³

§12 Remember the words of Almighty God: "You were looking to the battle before you engaged in it, and now you see it with your own two eyes." Remember: "How many small groups beat big groups by the will of God."⁴ And His words: "If God gives you victory, no one can beat you. And if He betrays you, who can give you victory without Him? So the faithful put their trust in God."⁵

§13 Remind yourself of the supplications and of your brethren and ponder their meanings. (The morning and evening supplications, and the supplications of [entering] a town, and the [unclear] supplications, and the supplications said before meeting the enemy.)

§14 Bless your body with some verses of the Qur'an [done by reading verses into one's hands and then rubbing the hands over whatever is to be blessed], the luggage, clothes, the knife, your personal effects, your ID, passport, and all your papers.

§15 Check your weapon before you leave and long before you leave. (You must make your knife sharp and must not discomfort your animal during the slaughter.)

§16 Tighten your clothes [a reference to making sure his clothes will cover his private parts at all times], since this is the way of the pious generations after the Prophet. They would tighten their clothes before battle. Tighten your shoes well, wear socks so that your feet will be solidly in your shoes. All of these are worldly things [that humans can do to control their fate, although God decrees what will work and what won't] and the rest is left to God, the best One to depend on.

§17 Pray the morning prayer in a group and ponder the great rewards of that prayer. Make supplications afterwards, and do not leave your apartment unless you have performed ablution before leaving, because the angels will ask for your forgiveness as long as you are in a state of ablution, and will pray for you. This saying of the Prophet was mentioned by An-Nawawi in his book, *The Best of Supplications*. Read the words of God: "Did you think that We created you for no reason . . . " from the Al-Mu'minun Chapter.[6]

THE SECOND STEP

§18 When the taxi takes you to (M) [this initial could stand for *matar*, airport in Arabic] remember God constantly while in the car. (Remember the supplication for entering a car, for entering a town, the supplication of place and other supplications.)

§19 When you have reached (M) and have left the taxi, say a supplication of place ["Oh Lord, I ask you for the best of this place, and ask you to protect me from its evils"], and everywhere you go say that prayer and smile and be calm, for God is with the believers. And the angels protect you without you feeling anything. Say this supplication: "God is more dear than all of His creation." And say: "Oh Lord, protect me from them as You wish." And say: "Oh Lord, take your anger out on [the enemy] and we ask You to protect us from their evils." And say: "Oh Lord, block their vision from in front of them, so that they may not see." And say: "God is all we need, He is the best to rely upon." Remember God's words: "Those to whom the people said, 'The people have gathered to get you, so fear them,' but that only increased their faith and they said, God is all we need, He is the best to rely upon."[7] After you say that, you will find [unclear] as God promised this to his servants who say this supplication:

1) They will come back [from battle] with God's blessings

2) They were not harmed

3) And God was satisfied with them.[8]

§20 God says: "They came back with God's blessings, were not harmed, and God was satisfied with them, and God is ever-blessing."[9]

§21 All of their equipment and gates and technology will not prevent, nor harm, except by God's will. The believers do not fear such things. The only ones that fear it are the allies of Satan, who are the brothers of the devil. They have become their allies, God save us, for fear is a great form of worship, and the only one worthy of it is God. He is the only one who deserves it. He said in the verses: "This is only the Devil scaring his allies"[10] who are fascinated with Western civilisation, and have drank the love [of the West] like they drink water [unclear] and have become afraid of their weak equipment, "so fear them not, and fear Me, if you are believers."[11]

§22 Fear is a great worship. The allies of God do not offer such worship except for the one God, who controls everything. [unclear] with total certainty that God will weaken the schemes of non-believers. God said: "God will weaken the schemes of the non-believers."[12]

§23 You must remember your brothers with all respect. No one should notice that you are making the supplication, "There is no God but God," because if you say it 1,000 times no one will be able to tell whether you are quiet or remember God. And among its miracles is what the Prophet, peace be upon him, said: "Whoever says, 'There is no God but God,' with all his heart, goes to heaven." The prophet, peace be upon him, said: "If you put all the worlds and universes on one side of the balance, and 'No God but God' on the other, 'No God but God' will weigh more heavily." You can repeat these words confidently, and this is just one of the strengths of these words. Whoever thinks deeply about these words will find that they have no dots [in the Arabic letter] and this is just one of its greatnesses, for words that have dots in them carry less weight than those that do not. And it is enough that these are the words of monotheism, which will make you steadfast in battle [unclear] as the prophet, peace be upon him, and his companions, and those who came after them, God willing, until the Day of Judgment.

§24 Do not seem confused or show signs of nervous tension. Be happy, optimistic, calm because you are heading for a deed that God loves and will accept. It will be the day, God willing, you spend with the women of paradise.

§25 [poetry] Smile in the face of hardship young man / For you are heading toward eternal paradise

§26 You must remember to make supplications wherever you go, and anytime you do anything, and God is with his faithful servants, He will protect them and make their tasks easier, and give them success and control, and victory, and everything . . .

THE THIRD PHASE

§27 When you ride the (T) [probably for *tayyara*, airplane in Arabic], before your foot steps in it, and before you enter it, you make a prayer and supplications. Remember that this is a battle for the sake of God. As the prophet, peace be upon him, said, "An action for the sake of God is better than all of what is in this world." When you step inside the (T), and sit in your seat, begin with the known supplications that we have mentioned before. Be busy with the constant remembrance of God. God said: "Oh ye faithful, when you find the enemy be steadfast, and remember God constantly so that you may be successful."[13] When the (T) moves, even slightly, toward (Q) [unknown reference], say the supplication of travel. Because you are traveling to Almighty God, so be attentive on this trip.

§28 Then [unclear] it takes off. This is the moment that both groups come together.[14] So remember God, as He said in His book: "Oh Lord, pour your patience upon us and make our feet steadfast and give us victory over the infidels."[15] And His words: "And the only thing they said Lord, forgive our sins and excesses and make our feet steadfast and give us victory over the infidels."[16] And His prophet said: "Oh Lord, You have revealed the book, You move the clouds, You gave us victory over the enemy, conquer them and give us victory over them." Give us victory and make the ground shake under their feet. Pray for yourself and all your brothers that they may be victorious and hit their targets and ask God to grant you martyrdom facing the enemy, not running away from it,[17] and for Him to grant you patience and the feeling that anything that happens to you is for Him.

§29 Then every one of you should prepare to carry out his role in a way that would satisfy God. You should clench your teeth, as the pious early generations did.

§30 When the confrontation begins, strike like champions who do not want to go back to this world. Shout, "Allahu Akbar," because this strikes fear in the hearts of the non-believers. God said: "Strike above the neck, and strike at all of their extremities."[18] Know that the gardens of paradise are waiting for you in all their beauty, and the women of paradise are waiting, calling out, "Come hither, friend of God." They have dressed in their most beautiful clothing.

§31 If God decrees that any of you are to slaughter, dedicate the slaughter to your fathers and [unclear], because you have obligations toward them. Do not disagree, and obey. If you slaughter, do not cause the discomfort of those you are killing, because this is one of the practices of the prophet, peace be upon him. On one condition: that you do not become distracted by [unclear] and neglect what is greater, paying attention to the enemy. That would be treason, and would do more damage than good. If this happens, the deed at hand is more important than doing that, because the deed is an obligation, and [the other thing] is optional. And an obligation has priority over an option.

§32 Do not seek revenge for yourself. Strike for God's sake. One time Ali bin Abi Talib [a companion and close relative of the prophet Muhammad], fought with a non-believer. The non-believer spit on Ali, may God bless him. Ali [unclear] his sword, but did not strike him. When the battle was over, the companions of the prophet asked him why he had not smitten the non-believer. He said, "After he spat at me, I was afraid I would be striking at him in revenge for myself, so I lifted my sword." After he renewed his intentions, he went back and killed the man. This means that before you do anything, make sure your soul is prepared to do everything for God only.

§33 Then implement the way of the prophet in taking prisoners. Take prisoners and kill them. As Almighty God said: "No prophet should have prisoners until he has soaked the land with blood. You want the bounties of this world [in exchange for prisoners] and God wants the other world [for you], and God is all-powerful, all-wise."[19]

§34 If everything goes well, every one of you should pat the other on the shoulder in confidence that (M) and (T) number (K). Remind your brothers that this act is for Almighty God. Do not confuse your brothers or distract them. He should give them glad tidings and make them calm, and remind them [of God] and encourage them. How beautiful it is for one to read God's words, such as: "And those who prefer the afterlife over this world should fight for the sake of God."[20] And His words: "Do not suppose that those who are killed for the sake of God are dead; they are alive . . . "[21] And others. Or they should sing songs to boost their morale, as the pious first generations did in the throes of battle, to bring calm, tranquillity and joy to the hearts of his brothers.

§35 Do not forget to take a bounty, even if it is a glass of water to quench your thirst or that of your brothers, if possible. When the hour of reality approaches, the zero hour, [unclear] and wholeheartedly welcome death for the sake of God. Always be remembering God. Either end your life while praying, seconds before the target, or make your last words: "There is no God but God, Muhammad is His messenger."

§36 Afterwards, we will all meet in the highest heaven, God willing.

§37 If you see the enemy as strong, remember the groups [that had formed a coalition to fight the prophet Muhammad]. They were 10,000. Remember how God gave victory to his faithful servants. He said: "When the faithful saw the groups, they said, this is what God and the prophet promised, they said the truth. It only increased their faith."[22]

§38 And may the peace of God be upon the prophet.

George W. Bush, Address to the Nation, October 7, 2001

§1 Good afternoon. On my orders the United States military has begun strikes against al Qaeda terrorist training camps and military installations of the Taliban regime in Afghanistan.[1]

§2 These carefully targeted actions are designed to disrupt the use of Afghanistan as a terrorist base of operations, and to attack the military capability of the Taliban regime.

§3 We are joined in this operation by our staunch friend, Great Britain. Other close friends, including Canada, Australia, Germany and France, have pledged forces as the operation unfolds.

§4 More than 40 countries in the Middle East, Africa, Europe and across Asia have granted air transit or landing rights. Many more have shared intelligence. We are supported by the collective will of the world.

§5 More than two weeks ago, I gave Taliban leaders a series of clear and specific demands: Close terrorist training camps; hand over leaders of the al Qaeda network; and return all foreign nationals, including American citizens, unjustly detained in your country. None of these demands were met. And now the Taliban will pay a price.

§6 By destroying camps and disrupting communication, we will make it more difficult for the terror network to train new recruits and coordinate their evil plans. Initially, the terrorists may burrow deeper into caves and other entrenched hiding places. Our military action is also designed to clear the way for sustained, comprehensive and relentless operations to drive them out and bring them to justice.

§7 At the same time, the oppressed people of Afghanistan will know the generosity of America and our allies. As we strike military targets, we will also drop food, medicine and supplies to the starving and suffering men and women and children of Afghanistan.

§8 The United States of America is a friend to the Afghan people. And we are the friends of almost a billion worldwide who practice the Islamic faith.

§9 The United States of America is an enemy of those who aid terrorists and of the barbaric criminals who profane a great religion by committing murder in its name.

§10 This military action is a part of our campaign against terrorism, another front in a war that has already been joined through diplomacy, intelligence, the freezing of financial assets and the arrests of known terrorists by law enforcement agents in 38 countries.

§11 Given the nature and reach of our enemies, we will win this conflict by the patient accumulation of successes, by meeting a series of challenges with determination and will and purpose.

§12 Today we focus on Afghanistan, but the battle is broader. Every nation has a choice to make. In this conflict, there is no neutral ground. If any government sponsors the outlaws and killers of innocents, they have become outlaws and murderers, themselves. And they will take that lonely path at their own peril.

§13 I'm speaking to you today from the Treaty Room of the White House, a place where American Presidents have worked for peace. We're a peaceful nation. Yet, as we have learned, so suddenly and so tragically, there can be no peace in a world of sudden terror. In the face of today's new threat, the only way to pursue peace is to pursue those who threaten it.

§14 We did not ask for this mission, but we will fulfill it. The name of today's military operation is Enduring Freedom. We defend not only our precious freedoms, but also the freedom of people everywhere to live and raise their children free from fear.

§15 I know many Americans feel fear today. And our government is taking strong precautions. Our law enforcement and intelligence agencies are working aggressively around America, around the world and around the clock. At my request, many governors have activated the National Guard to strengthen airport security. We have called up Reserves to reinforce our military capability and strengthen the protection of our homeland.

§16 In the months ahead, our patience will be one of our strengths—patience with the long waits that will result from tighter security; patience and understanding that it will take time to achieve our goals; patience in all the sacrifices that may come.

§17 Today, those sacrifices are being made by members of our Armed Forces who now defend us so far from home, and by their proud and worried families.

§18 A Commander-in-Chief sends America's sons and daughters into a battle in a foreign land only after the greatest care and a lot of prayer. We ask a lot of those who wear our uniform. We ask them to leave their loved ones, to travel great distances, to risk injury, even to be prepared to make the ultimate sacrifice of their lives. They are dedicated; they are honorable; they represent the best of our country. And we are grateful.

§19 To all the men and women in our military—every sailor, every soldier, every airman, every coast guardsman, every marine—I say this:

§20 Your mission is defined; your objectives are clear; your goal is just. You have my full confidence, and you will have every tool you need to carry out your duty.

§21 I recently received a touching letter that says a lot about the state of America in these difficult times—a letter from a 4th-grade girl, with a father in the military. "As much as I don't want my Dad to fight," she wrote, "I'm willing to give him to you." This is a precious gift, the greatest she could give. This young girl knows what America is all about.

§22 Since September 11, an entire generation of young Americans has gained new understanding of the value of freedom, and its cost in duty and in sacrifice.

§23 The battle is now joined on many fronts. We will not waver; we will not tire; we will not falter; and we will not fail. Peace and freedom will prevail. Thank you. May God continue to bless America.

Osama bin Laden, Videotaped Address, October 7, 2001

§1 Here is America struck by God Almighty in one of its vital organs, so that its greatest buildings are destroyed. Grace and gratitude to God. America has been filled with horror from north to south and east to west, and thanks be to God. What America is tasting now is only a copy of what we have tasted.[1]

§2 Our Islamic nation has been tasting the same for more than 80 years of humiliation and disgrace, its sons killed and their blood spilled, its sanctities desecrated.

§3 God has blessed a group of vanguard Muslims, the forefront of Islam, to destroy America. May God bless them and allot them a supreme place in heaven, for he is the only one capable and entitled to do so. When those have stood in defense of their weak children, their brothers and sisters in Palestine and other Muslim nations, the whole world went into an uproar, the infidels followed by the hypocrites.

§4 A million innocent children are dying at this time as we speak, killed in Iraq without any guilt. We hear no denunciation, we hear no edict from the hereditary rulers. In these days, Israeli tanks rampage across Palestine, in Ramallah, Rafah and Beit Jala and many other parts of the land of Islam [dar al-Islam], and we do not hear anyone raising his voice or reacting. But when the sword fell upon America after 80 years, hypocrisy raised its head up high bemoaning those killers who toyed with the blood, honor and sanctities of Muslims.

§5 The least that can be said about those hypocrites is that they are apostates who followed the wrong path. They backed the butcher against the victim, the oppressor against the innocent child. I seek refuge in God against them and ask him to let us see them in what they deserve.

§6 I say that the matter is very clear. Every Muslim, after this event, after the senior officials in the United States of America starting with the head of international infidels. Bush and his staff who went on a display of vanity with their men and horses, those who turned even the countries that believe in Islam against us—the group that resorted to God, the Almighty, the group that refuses to be subdued in its religion.

§7 They have been telling the world falsehoods that they are fighting terrorism. In a nation at the far end of the world, Japan, hundreds of thousands, young and old, were killed and this is not a world crime. To them it is not a clear issue. A million children in Iraq, to them this is not a clear issue.

§8 But when a few more than 10 were killed in Nairobi and Dar es Salaam, Afghanistan and Iraq were bombed and hypocrisy stood behind the head of international infidels: the modern world's symbol of paganism, America, and its allies.

§9 I tell them that these events have divided the world into two camps, the camp of the faithful and the camp of infidels. May God shield us and you from them.

§10 Every Muslim must rise to defend his religion. The wind of faith is blowing and the wind of change is blowing to remove evil from the Peninsula of Muhammad, peace be upon him.

§11 As to America, I say to it and its people a few words: I swear to God that America will not live in peace before peace reigns in Palestine, and before all the army of infidels depart the land of Muhammad, peace be upon him.

§12 God is the greatest and glory be to Islam.

Transcript of Pat Robertson's Interview with Jerry Falwell
Broadcast on the 700 Club, September 13, 2001

¶1 PAT ROBERTSON: And we have thought that we're invulnerable. And we have been so concerned about money. We have been so concerned about material things. The interests of people are on their health and their finances, and on their pleasures and on their sexuality, and while this is going on while we're self-absorbed and the churches as well as in the population, we have allowed rampant pornography on the internet. We have allowed rampant secularism and occult, etc. to be broadcast on television. We have permitted somewhere in the neighborhood of 35 to 40 million unborn babies to be slaughtered in our society. We have a court that has essentially stuck its finger in God's eye and said we're going to legislate you out of the schools. We're going to take your commandments from off the courthouse steps in various states. We're not going to let little children read the commandments of God. We're not going to let the Bible be read, no prayer in our schools. We have insulted God at the highest levels of our government. And, then we say "why does this happen?"

¶2 Well, why it's happening is that God Almighty is lifting his protection from us. And once that protection is gone, we all are vulnerable because we're a free society, and we're vulnerable. We lay naked before these terrorists who have infiltrated our country. There's probably tens of thousands of them in America right now. They've been raising money. They've been preaching their hate and overseas they have been spewing out venom against the United States for years. All over the Arab world, there is venom being poured out into people's ears and minds against America. And, the only thing that's going to sustain us is the umbrella power of the Almighty God.

[Break]

¶3 PAT ROBERTSON: Well, after Tuesday's attacks, many Americans are struggling with grief, fear and unanswered questions. How should Christians respond to this crisis? Well, joining us now with some answers is a dear friend of ours, the Pastor of the Thomas Road Baptist Church and Liberty

University, the head and founder of that, Dr. Jerry Falwell. Jerry, it's a delight to have you with us today.

§4 JERRY FALWELL: Thanks, Pat.

§5 PAT ROBERTSON: Listen. What are you telling the church? You called your church together. What was your response at Thomas Road to this tragedy?

§6 JERRY FALWELL: Well, as the world knows, the tragedy hit on Tuesday morning, and at 2:00 in the afternoon, we gathered 7,000 Liberty University students, faculty, local people together, and we used the verse that I heard you use a moment ago, Chronicles II, 7:14, that God wanted us to humble ourselves and seek his face. And there's not much we can do in the Church but what we're supposed to do, and that is pray. Pray for the President that God will give him wisdom, keep bad advisors from him, bring good ones to him, praying for the families of the victims, praying for America. And, you know this thing is not a great deal different than what I remember and you, Pat. We're about the same age. December 7, 1941, when we entered the war against Japan, Germany, Italy. Hitler's goal was to destroy the Jews among other things, and conquer the world. And, these Islamic fundamentalists, these radical terrorists, these Middle Eastern monsters are committed to destroying the Jewish nation, driving her into the Mediterranean, conquering the world. And, we are the great Satan. We are the ultimate goal. I talked this morning with Tom Rose, publisher of the *Jerusalem Post,* and orthodox Jew, and he said, "Now America knows in a horrible way what Israel's been facing for 53 years at the hand of Arafat and other terrorists and radicals and barbarians.

§7 PAT ROBERTSON: Jerry, I know that you shared several 40-day fasts for revival in America. We here at CBN had a couple of 40-day fasts during the Lenten season, and Bill Bright, I don't know, eight or nine.[1] Do you think that this is going to be the trigger of revival, a real revival in the Church where we truly turn back to God with all our heart?

§8 JERRY FALWELL: It could be. I've never sensed a togetherness, a burden, a broken heart[2] as I do in the Church today, and just 48 hours, I gave away a booklet I wrote 10 years ago. I gave it away last night on the Biblical position on fasting and prayer because I do believe that that is what we've got to do now—fast and pray. And I agree totally with you that the Lord has protected us so wonderfully these 225 years. And since 1812, this is the first time that we've been attacked on our soil, first time, and by far the worst results. And I fear, as Donald Rumsfeld, the Secretary of Defense said yesterday, that this is only the beginning. And with biological warfare available to these monsters; the Husseins, the Bin Ladens, the Arafats, what we saw on Tuesday, as terrible as it is, could be miniscule if, in fact, if in fact God continues to lift the curtain and allow the enemies of America to give us probably what we deserve.

§9 PAT ROBERTSON: Jerry, that's my feeling. I think we've just seen the antechamber to terror. We haven't even begun to see what they can do to the major population.

§10 JERRY FALWELL: The ACLU's got to take a lot of blame for this.

§11 PAT ROBERTSON: Well, yes.

§12 JERRY FALWELL: And, I know that I'll hear from them for this. But, throwing God out successfully with the help of the federal court system, throwing God out of the public square, out of the schools. The abortionists have got to bear some burden for this because God will not be mocked. And when we destroy 40 million little innocent babies, we make God mad. I really believe that the pagans, and the abortionists, and the feminists, and the gays and the lesbians who are actively trying to make that an alternative lifestyle, the ACLU, People For the American Way, all of them who have tried to secularize America. I point the finger in their face and say: "You helped this happen."

§13 PAT ROBERTSON: Well, I totally concur, and the problem is we have adopted that agenda at the highest levels of our government. And so we're responsible as a free society for what the top people do. And, the top people, of course, is the court system.

§14 JERRY FALWELL: Amen. Pat, did you notice yesterday? The ACLU, and all the Christ-haters, the People For the American Way, NOW, etc. were totally disregarded by the Democrats and the Republicans in both houses of Congress as they went out on the steps and called out on to God in prayer and sang "God Bless America" and said: "Let the ACLU be hanged!" In other words, when the nation is on its knees, the only normal and natural and spiritual thing to do is what we ought to be doing all the time—calling upon God.

§15 PAT ROBERTSON: Amen. I wanted to ask you the reaction. I know that you had a major prayer meeting last night, and I know your people assembled, just a large gathering at your church. What was the mood of the people? What did they say and what did you sense with your congregation?

§16 JERRY FALWELL: A brokenness that I have not seen. I've been their pastor 45 years, 30 years Chancellor at Liberty. We had 7,000 gather yesterday in the Vines Center and filled the Church last night. I sensed a brokenness, tears. People were sobbing at the altar. And, they have no shame about it. It was the kind of brokenness that no one could conjure, only God could bring upon us. And, that is to me the most optimistic thing that I see today as I look across America. And every city, I called a friend in Springfield yesterday. He said at least a hundred churches, Springfield, MO, at least a hundred churches have special prayer meetings for America today and tonight. And, that's happening by the thousands all over America. This could be, if we will fast and pray, this could be God's call to revival.

§17 PAT ROBERTSON: Well, I believe it. And I think the people, the Bible says render your hearts and not your garments, and people begin to render their hearts and they weep before the Lord, and they really get serious with God, God will hear and answer. We'll see revival. I am thrilled to hear that about your church because it's happening all over.

§18 JERRY FALWELL: It's everywhere.

§19 PAT ROBERTSON: Yes.

§20 JERRY FALWELL: In the most unlikely of places. The general manager at the ABC affiliate in our area called me this morning and said: "We're going to ask for all the churches, all the people of faith to join us at the D-Day Memorial over in Bedford at 2:00, Sunday. And, Randy Smith is his name, the general manager, and he is calling central Virginia to healing through prayer and I suspect there will be thousands there.

§21 PAT ROBERTSON: Jerry, this is so encouraging, and I thank God for your stand. We just love you and praise God for you. Liberty is a great institution and I congratulate you for that wonderful student body, and your church. And, thank you, my dear friend, for being with us.

§22 JERRY FALWELL: God bless you, brother. Let's stand together.

§23 PAT ROBERTSON: Amen.

CHAPTER ONE

Lecture first presented at the University of Copenhagen, November 14, 2001, subsequently offered at the University of Colorado, Department of Religious Studies, and the University of California, Santa Cruz, Program in History of Consciousness.

1. Clifford Geertz, "Religion as a Cultural System," *The Interpretation of Cultures* (New York: Basic Books, 1973), p. 90; first published in *Anthropological Approaches to the Study of Religion*, ed. Michael Banton (London: Tavistock, 1966).

2. Talal Asad, *Genealogies of Religion: Discipline and Reasons of Power in Christianity and Islam* (Baltimore: Johns Hopkins University Press, 1993), esp. chap. 1 ("The Construction of Religion as an Anthropological Category," pp. 27–54). This was first published in *Man* (1983) but was more widely read and acquired more force when combined with the other materials in this book. It is surely no accident that in two different generations, the most telling critiques of attempts to define "religion" have come from scholars primarily concerned with Islam, who perceive the discriminatory features of others' formulations. Thus, Wilfred Cantwell Smith, *The Meaning and End of Religion: A New Approach to the Religious Traditions of Mankind* (New York: Macmillan, 1963), in appreciation and critical response to which, see Talal Asad, "Reading a Modern Classic: W. C. Smith's *The Meaning and End of Religion*," *History of Religions* 40 (2001): 205–22.

3. Peter Gay, *The Enlightenment: An Interpretation*. Vol. 1: *The Rise of Modern Paganism;* Vol. 2: *The Science of Freedom* (New York: W. W. Norton, 1966–69).

4. Kant treats these issues most explicitly in *Religion within the Limits of Reason Alone* (1793), although he approaches it more obliquely in earlier writings. Asad deals with Kant on several occasions but does not cite this work directly, preferring to focus his attention on the 1784 essay "An Answer to the Question: What Is Enlightenment?" and the *Critique of Pure Reason* (*Genealogies of Religion*, pp. 41–43, 201–8, 227–28).

5. Asad, *Genealogies of Religion*, p. 29.

6. A recent exception is Pascal Boyer, *Religion Explained: The Human Instincts that Fashion Gods, Spirits and Ancestors* (London: Heinemann, 2001), which builds on his earlier *The Naturalness of Religious Ideas: A Cognitive Theory of Religion* (Berkeley: University of California Press, 1994). The latter volume seems to have been under way before Asad's critique gained currency; likewise, E. Thomas Lawson and Robert N. McCauley, *Rethinking Religion: Connecting Cognition and Culture* (Cambridge: Cambridge University Press, 1990); and Stewart Guthrie, *Faces in the Clouds: A New Theory of Religion* (New York: Oxford University Press, 1993).

7. William Shepard, *Sayyid Qutb and Islamic Activism: A Translation and Critical Analysis of "Social Justice in Islam"* (Leiden: Brill, 1996), p. 1. *Social Justice in Islam*, Qutb's first major work, was initially published in 1949. Subsequent editions, particularly those of 1958 and 1964, show substantial revision, reflecting Qutb's increasingly Islamist views. Shepard's translation is based

on the 1964 edition but discusses the process of revision. An English translation of the first edition is also available: Sayyid Qutb, *Social Justice in Islam*, trans. John Hardie, rev. by Hamid Algar (Oneonta, N.Y.: Islamic Publications International, 2000).

8. The fullest discussion of Qutb's time in the United States is John Calvert's "'The World Is an Undutiful Boy!': Sayyid Qutb's American Experience," *Islam and Christian-Muslim Relations* 11, no. 1 (March 2000): 87–103. Also useful are Ahmed Salah al-Din Mousalli, *Radical Islamic Fundamentalism: The Ideological and Political Discourse of Sayyid Qutb* (Beirut: American University of Beirut, 1992), especially chap. 1; and Ibrahim Abu-Rabi', *Intellectual Origins of Islamic Resurgence in the Modern Arab World* (Albany: State University of New York Press, 1996), pp. 92–137.

9. With regard to this concept, I have benefited from reading an unpublished paper by William Shepard, "Jahiliyyah in the Thought of Sayyid Qutb," presented at annual meetings of the American Research Center in Egypt (Chicago, April 23–25, 1999). The most important and frequently cited of Qutb's later work is his *Ma'alim fi al-tariq*, usually translated *Milestones*, as in the revised English translation by Ahmad Zaki Hammad (Indianapolis: American Trust Publications, 1990). In the introduction to that work, he explicates the nature of *Jahiliyyah* and constitutes a maximalist view of Islam as its antithesis and unique antidote.

> If we look at the sources and foundations of modern ways of living, it becomes clear that the whole world is steeped in *jahiliyyah* [ignorance of the divine guidance], and all the marvellous material comforts and high-level inventions do not diminish this ignorance. This *jahiliyyah* is based on rebellion against God's sovereignty on earth. It transfers to man one of the greatest attributes of God, namely sovereignty, and makes some men lords over others. It is now not in that simple and primitive form of the ancient *jahiliyyah*, but takes the form of claiming that the right to create values, to legislate rules of collective behavior, and to choose any way of life rests with men, without regard to what God has prescribed. The result of this rebellion against the authority of God is the oppression of His creatures. . . . In this respect, Islam's way of life is unique, for in systems other than Islam, some people worship others in some form or another. Only in the Islamic way of life do all men become free from the servitude of some men to others and devote themselves to the worship of God alone, deriving guidance from Him alone, and bowing before Him alone. This is where the roads separate. . . . (pp. 8–9)

10. It is useful to cite Calvert's description of Greeley, a community of twenty thousand at the time: "Established as a self-declared utopian community in 1870, the city proudly maintained in the late 1940s the moral rigor, temperance and civic-mindedness that were the hallmarks of its founding fathers. . . . Greeley's first settlers had imposed a total ban on alcohol which was still in effect during Qutb's stay. In the minds of many Americans in the postwar era, the qualities of Greeley represented the best the United States had to offer" (Calvert, "'The World Is an Undutiful Boy!'" p. 95).

11. This passage, which has been frequently cited, initially appeared in the second of three articles Qutb published upon his return to Egypt, entitled "Amerika alladhī ra'ayt: Fīmīzān al-qiyam al-insāniyyah—2" ["The America I Saw: Weighed in the Balance of Human Values, Part 2"] *al-Risalah* Year 19, vol. 2, no. 959 (November 19, 1951), p. 1304. The translation I have quoted comes from Robert Worth, "The Deep Intellectual Roots of Islamic Terror," *New York Times*, October 13, 2001, p. A15.

12. Regarding Qutb's broader thought on this topic, I have benefited from William Shepard, "Gender Relations in the Thought of Sayyid Qutb," unpublished paper presented at meetings of the Middle East Studies Association (December 1995).

13. Quoted in Mousalli, *Radical Islamic Fundamentalism,* pp. 26–27. In the subsequent discussion, Qutb assesses why the disjuncture between the religious and the social was evident in the events he observed at Greeley.

> Nothing in this is strange because the priest does not feel that his job is different from that of a stage manager or store manager. Success is first and prior to anything else. Means are unimportant; for success brings him good consequences: money and prestige. The greater the number of church-goers, the greater his income, prestige, and influence in the town. (Ibid., pp. 27–28)

14. There is a large, extremely uneven literature on the topic of "fundamentalism." The best works include Martin Riesebrodt, *Pious Passions: The Emergence of Modern Fundamentalism in the United States and Iran* (Berkeley: University of California Press, 1993); Bruce Lawrence, *Defenders of God: The Fundamentalist Revolt against the Modern Age* (Columbia: University of South Carolina Press, 1995); and Roxanne Euben, *Enemy in the Mirror: Islamic Fundamentalism and the Limits of Modern Rationalism: A Work of Comparative Political Theory* (Princeton: Princeton University Press, 1999). The connotations of this term have become so strong, however, that I think it preferable to avoid it altogether.

15. My preference for "discourse" over "belief" is based on two arguments. First is an epistemological consideration. Students of religion have no unmediated access to the beliefs of those they study, nor to any other aspects of their interiority. Rather, we come to know something of those beliefs only as they find external (always imperfect and sometimes quite distorted) expression in acts of discourse and practice. Regarding that of which one can have no direct knowledge, scholars cannot speak with any confidence and should—in their professional capacity, at least—perforce remain silent. Second, an ontological and ontogenetic observation: Belief almost never arises de novo in pristine interior reflection and experience, but generally follows exposure to the discourse of significant others. These include parents, above all, but also friends, family, and clergy, who signal what they believe and what they (also the institutions and traditions to which they belong) believe ought be believed. As these statements are received and metabolized by those to whom they are addressed, they are internalized as beliefs, but in this process, discourse is both logically and chronologically prior to belief.

16. Heuristically clear, the line between religious and nonreligious discourse may become blurred in practice, as when speakers make claim to absolute truths without explicit gestures to the transcendent, as in the case of Marxists with extreme confidence in historic dialectics. Buddhism offers another instructive example. Insofar as the teachings of the Buddha are constituted as something achieved through the most serious, sustained reflection undertaken by the most gifted of all sentient beings—but someone regarded as still human—these remain the basis of a philosophy and not a religion. When those same teachings are represented as the product of a person and/or process more than human in nature, Buddhism has taken the first and most important step to reformulating itself as a religion. Similar points can be made about varying forms of nationalism.

17. On September 11 Mohamed Atta took two flights, one from Maine to Boston and the second from Boston to Los Angeles (American Airlines Flight 11). In Maine he checked his baggage through only as far as Boston, where it remained until discovered. Although other explanations are possible (an error made in haste, perhaps), it seems most likely that he intended for the

suitcase to be discovered, so that the instructions and his will (drafted in April 1996) would be read and supply others with the basis for interpreting his life and final actions. The will contains eighteen numbered items, all of which assert his identity as a good Muslim. The original Arabic text has never been released, and only translated excerpts appeared in the American press. A full translation in German was published in *Der Spiegel*, October 1, 2001. An English translation from this German text may be found at http://abcnews.go.com/sections/us/dailynews/ WTC_atta_will.html.

18. The second copy to be recovered was found in the vehicle used by Nawaf Alhazmi before he boarded American Airlines Flight 77 in Washington, and the third at the crash site of United Airlines Flight 93 in Stony Creek Township, Pennsylvania. Facsimiles of the original Arabic holograph were made available by the FBI at www.fbi.gov/pressrel/pressrel01/letter.htm. Although press reports consistently referred to a five-page document, the FBI website reproduced only four, the first page of the original apparently having been withheld.

19. Three authoritative oral traditions (*hadith*) are also introduced, always framed as words of the Prophet (§§23, 27, 28).

20. Sura 9.12–14; my emphasis. Cf. the use of Scripture in §30: "When the confrontation begins, strike like champions who do not want to go back to this world. Shout, 'Allahu Akbar,' because this strikes fear in the hearts of the non-believers. God said: 'Strike above the neck, and strike at all of their extremities.'" The Quranic passage cited is sura 8.12–14, which reads as follows:

> When the Lord was revealing to the angels,
> "I am with you; so confirm the believers.
> I shall cast into the unbelievers' hearts
> Terror; *so smite above the necks, and smite every finger of them!*"
> That, because they had made a breach
> with God and with His Messenger; and
> whosoever makes a breach with God and with
> His Messenger, surely God is terrible in retribution.
> That for you; therefore taste it; and
> That the chastisement of the Fire is for the unbelievers (my emphasis).

The promise of chastisement by fire for unbelievers is especially ominous when set in homologic relation to events of September 11.

21. Qutb, *Milestones*, pp. 38–40. See further the discussion of Shepard, "Jahiliyyah in the Thought of Sayyid Qutb," pp. 12–15.

22. This is not to say their motives were exclusively religious. Anger over American foreign policy toward Palestine and Iraq, for instance, surely played some role in prompting the attacks of September 11. Here, however, I would make two points: (1) Such considerations go completely unmentioned in the instructions text (perhaps because they are taken for granted); and (2) in other texts where they do enter, the discourse itself conflates "religious" and "political" aspects, which can only be separated by an outside observer insensitive to their intimate interrelation. Thus, to pursue the example, "Palestine" and "Iraq" do not figure simply as nation-states and political entities. Rather, they are of concern precisely because they are Muslim nations or, more simply, part of "Islam" (*dar al-Islam*, on the significance of which, see the discussion in chapter 3).

23. This, of course, is a classic theme, treated not only in Kant's *Religion within the Limits of Reason Alone*, but also in different ways and to different purposes in Kierkegaard's *Fear and Trem-*

bling, Dostoyevsky's *Brothers Karamazov,* and Nietzsche's *Genealogy of Morals.* Professional students of religion have often been a good deal more superficial in treating the issues raised by such troubling practices as collective suicide, spousal immolation, and clitoridectomy, where they can usually be counted on to smooth out the apparent contradiction between the ethical and the religious. Toward that end, scholars who harbor a distinctly nonacademic reverence for their object of study can be counted on to deploy one of two favored arguments: (1) It is ethnocentric to ignore or undervalue the profound significance these practices have in their proper cultural context (i.e., being religious, they must be good); and (2) the perpetrators are frauds, hypocrites, dupes, or members of "cults" (i.e., being bad, they can't *really* be religious). In either case, the goal is the same and the project transparently apologetic.

24. For summary discussions of these and other related figures, see Ali Rahnema, ed., *Pioneers of Islamic Revival* (London: Zed Books, 1994). Specifically on the Muslim Brotherhood, see Richard P. Mitchell, *The Society of the Muslim Brothers* (Oxford: Oxford University Press, 1993; 1st ed. 1969).

25. §21 of the instructions draws a related contrast between those whose strength is grounded in religious faith and those who depend on technology.

> All of their equipment and gates and technology will not prevent, nor harm, except by God's will. The believers do not fear such things. The only ones that fear it are the allies of Satan, who are the brothers of the devil. They have become their allies, God save us, for fear is a great form of worship, and the only one worthy of it is God. He is the only one who deserves it. He said in the verses: "This is only the Devil scaring his allies," who are fascinated with Western civilisation, and have drank the love [of the West] like they drink water [unclear] and have become afraid of their weak equipment, "so fear them not, and fear Me, if you are believers."

26. Cf. Mark Juergensmeyer's discussion of the theatricality of much religio-political violence, in *Terror in the Mind of God: The Global Rise of Religious Violence* (Berkeley: University of California Press, 2000), pp. 119–44.

CHAPTER TWO

First presented at the University of Chicago, M.A. Program in Social Sciences, October 22, 2001, pieces of which were published as "The Other War: The One of Words," *Kansas City Star,* October 23, 2001, available at www.kcstar.com/item/pages/opinion.pat,opinion/3acd143c.a23,.html. Later versions were presented to the History of Religions workshop at the University of Chicago and a conference on "Apocalypticism and Violence" organized at Yale University.

1. Paul Farhi, "The Networks, Giving Aid to the Enemy?" *Washington Post,* October 12, 2001, p. C1.

2. I mean this term in its strictly Nietzschean sense, as developed in the *Genealogy of Morals,* with particular reference to the priestly perspective.

3. The genealogy of this stereotype can be traced at least to the Mahdist insurrection of 1884–85 in the Anglo-Egyptian Sudan. When Muhammad Ahmad, self-proclaimed Mahdi (salvific hero), defeated the English army under General Charles Gordon and captured Khartoum, caricatures of extraordinary proportions were used to rally English popular opinion in the wake of this disaster.

4. The most important document is the "Declaration of War against the Americans Occupy-

ing the Land of the Two Holy Places" that bin Laden issued on behalf of al Qaeda in August 1996, available at www.chretiens-et-juifs.org/BIN_LADEN/Laden_war_amer.htm. These sentiments were repeated and amplified in the "Jihad against Jews and Crusaders World Islamic Front Statement" issued by bin Laden, Ayman al-Zawahiri, and others on February 23, 1998, available at www.chretiens-et-juifs.org/BIN_LADEN/Bin_Laden%27s_Fatwa_1998.htm. Also relevant are interviews bin Laden gave to various Western reporters in October–November 1996, available at www.islam.org.au/articles/15/LADIN.HTM; March 1997, available at www.anusha.com/osamaint.htm; May 1998, available at www.pbs.org/wgbh/pages/frontline/shows/binladen/who/interview.html; and later in 1998, available at www.ict.org.il/articles/bombings.cfm.

5. Prior to his October 7 address, bin Laden had spoken rather less about the Palestinian situation than he did on this occasion. Some have seen this shift as an opportunistic attempt to broaden his appeal and enlist sympathies throughout the Muslim world.

6. Women barely enter the speech of Bush or bin Laden, although either one might well have chosen to represent himself and his people as much more concerned with the welfare of women, albeit by radically different notions of what such welfare entails. Bin Laden was silent on the topic, while Bush made only two formulaic references to "the starving and suffering men and women and children of Afghanistan" (§7) and "the men and women in our military" (§19). That women are (minimally) present for Bush and absent for bin Laden is itself perhaps significant.

7. This announcement effectively withdrew the name given the mission in earlier statements: "Infinite Justice," a designation judged potentially offensive to Muslims. Since they take the infinite to be a property of God alone, it is presumptuous for humans to claim such status for their acts or values.

8. I do not mean to suggest that bin Laden was guilty of anything that could be interpreted as blasphemy. Rather, he played at the limits of the possible, without going over the line. At no point did he claim divine inspiration or overtly represent himself as a vehicle of revelation. Still, the force of his moral certainty, the violent judgments he called down on his enemies, and his ringing assertion "I say that the matter is very clear" (§6), when speaking of past, present, and future, all are hallmarks of prophetic discourse. In contrast, when Bush used a similar locution, it served to mark him as a resolute political leader, not an inspired prophet. "To all the men and women in our military—every sailor, every soldier, every airman, every coast guardsman, every marine—I say this: Your mission is defined; your objectives are clear; your goal is just" (§§19–20).

9. Both men preferred first-person plural pronouns to those of the first-person singular, Bush by a ratio of four to one (37:9) and bin Laden by two to one, although his frequency for both was much less (9:4). In contrast to Bush's opening assertion of his own authority ("On my orders . . . " [§1]), bin Laden began by describing events for which he took no personal credit but ascribed to God's will ("America has been filled with horror from north to south and east to west, and thanks be to God" [§1]).

10. Note the play of pronouns in §§13–18, where the initial distinction between first-person singular and second-person plural ("I'm speaking to you today" [§13]) dissolved into a cascade of first-person plurals encompassing—and more actively reconstituting—the American nation. Sixteen different first-person-plural pronouns occur in these paragraphs, beginning with a moment of national self-definition ("We're a peaceful nation" [§13]). Subsequently, there are assertions of collective resolve ("We did not ask for this mission, but we will fulfill it" [§14]) and an enumeration of responsible state organs ("Our government is taking strong precautions. Our law enforcement and intelligence agencies are working aggressively. . . . We have called up Re-

serves" [§15], "our Armed Forces who now defend us" [§17]), after which the military is hived off as a third-person "they" who defend the remaining "us" ("They are dedicated; they are honorable; they represent the best of our country. And we are grateful" [§18]).

11. On September 14 Bush described his anti-terrorist campaign as a "crusade . . . against a new kind of evil." This was widely reported and prompted so much adverse comment that four days later White House Press Secretary Ari Fleischer was forced to issue the following tortured explanation-*cum*-retraction. "To the degree that the word has any connotations that would upset any of our partners, or anybody else in the world, the president would regret if anything like that was conveyed. But the purpose of his conveying it is in the traditional English sense of the word. It's a broad cause" (Mike Conklin, "U.S. Spokesmen Stumble through Verbal Minefield," *Chicago Tribune*, November 1, 2001, sec. 5, p. 1). One also needs to evaluate Bush's denial that his policies are anti-Muslim in any measure vis-à-vis the concrete practices his administration has adopted, both international and domestic.

12. It is surely no accident that the Middle East was given first position in the list of regions from which logistical support had been obtained: "More than 40 countries in the Middle East, Africa, Europe and across Asia have granted air transit or landing rights. Many more have shared intelligence" (§4).

13. Samuel Huntington first published his views as an article, "The Clash of Civilizations," *Foreign Affairs* 72, no. 3 (1993): 22–49, with spirited responses by others following in vol. 72, no. 4: 2–9, 10–26, and vol. 72, no. 5: 186–94. An expanded version then came out in book form, Samuel P. Huntington, *The Clash of Civilizations and the Remaking of World Order* (New York: Simon & Schuster, 1996).

14. To this end, the United States was particularly eager to enlist Muslim states in the "anti-terrorist" campaign and to involve them in any way possible. The Turkish decision to send a token number of troops to Afghanistan was thus a welcome step, as was the statement of Prime Minister Bulent Ecevit: "Those who portray this campaign as an action against Islam are contradicting the high values of Islam, which is a religion of peace" (Douglas Frantz, "Turkey Says Elite Troops Will Join U.S. Campaign to Train Anti-Taliban Force," *New York Times*, November 2, 2001, p. B3). Turkey was the likeliest candidate to take such a step, and this for two reasons: (1) It is the sole Islamic nation to be a member of NATO and has consistently sought close political and economic relations with European powers; and (2) under the constitution introduced by Kemal Atatürk in 1923 and based on European models, the Turkish state was established as a secular republic, notwithstanding the Islamic identity of the nation. While this arrangement has been contested in recent years by political parties that advocate a religious state, it is defended, above all, by the military, whose officers understand themselves as Atatürk's heirs, protectors of his legacy and the institutional structures he founded.

15. The religious words and phrases in bin Laden's speech include the following: God (7 times); grace, Islam(ic) (5 times); Muslim(s) (5 times); bless(ed) (2 times); a supreme place in heaven, infidels (5 times); without any guilt, denunciation, edict (*fatwa*), hypocrisy, -ites (4 times); sanctities (2 times); desecrated, the land of Islam, apostates, the wrong path, refuge in God, what they deserve, believe, a display of vanity, the group that refuses to be subdued in its religion, paganism, the camp of the faithful, the wind of faith, I swear to God, Muhammad, peace be upon him (2 times); God is the greatest, glory be to Islam. Beyond this, one might also consider such phrases as "What America is tasting," "God . . . is the only one capable and entitled to do so," "defense of their weak children," "innocent children," "when the sword fell," "a display of vanity with their men and horses," etc.

16. Bush's text also includes several items that participate in religious (and more specifically biblical) discourse without being explicitly religious themselves. Along these lines, one might note "The ultimate sacrifice of their lives" (§18), "Your mission is defined" (§20), and, more broadly, the discussion of generosity in §7, that of patience in §16, or the rhythmic cadences of §23 that feel almost hymnodic: "We will not waver, we will not tire, we will not falter, and we will not fail." That such expressions have a broad range of semantics and can evoke divergent associations in different constituencies of a national audience is what makes them useful, as will shortly become apparent.

17. The importance of General Musharraf's position in bin Laden's analysis was underscored by a letter he released through al-Jazeera on November 1, in which he accused the Pakistani regime of "standing under the banner of the cross while Muslims are being slaughtered in Afghanistan." "Infidels" and "hypocrites" were again key terms in bin Laden's discourse, as he called for Muslim solidarity ("Supporters of Islam, this is the day to support Islam") and characterized American military action as a religious crusade ("The heat of the crusade against Islam has intensified, its ardor has increased, and the killing has multiplied against the followers of Muhammad") (Susan Sachs, "Bin Laden Letter Calls upon Pakistanis to Defend Islam," *New York Times*, November 2, 2001, p. B2).

18. Conceivably, an allusion to Joshua 10:16–26 may also be implicit, a story in which five Canaanite kings hide in a cave at Makkedah. Discovering this, the Israelites block the cave's entrance with heavy boulders, then defeat the kings' armies, take their cities, and return to deal with the kings, whom they humiliate and execute, but not before Joshua proclaims, "Do not be afraid or dismayed; be strong and of good courage; for thus the Lord will do to all your enemies against whom you fight" (10:25).

19. Also relevant are Job 24:13–14, Psalms 23:35, Psalms 25:4–5, Proverbs 1:15–16, and Proverbs 4:14–15, Isaiah 3:11–12, and others.

20. Bush's use of the phrase "killers of innocents" (§12) may reference this verse, also Exodus 23:7 ("Do not slay the innocent and righteous, for I will not acquit the wicked"), Deuteronomy 27:25 ("Cursed be he who takes a bribe to slay an innocent person"), and Psalms 10:7–8:

> His mouth is filled with cursing and deceit and oppression;
> under his tongue are mischief and iniquity.
> He sits in ambush in the villages;
> In hiding places he murders the innocent.

Finally, although the term itself does not appear in the biblical text, Herod's massacre of Israelite children, described in Matthew 2:16, conventionally called "the slaughter of the innocents," provides another clear point of reference.

21. Note also the discussion of patience in §16, with possible echoes of Psalm 37:7 and James 5:7–10, as well as the mention of "battle in a foreign land" (§18), with similar relation to I Chronicles 14:17.

22. Cf. the way those of somewhat different, New Age religious sensibilities quickly constituted the September 11 attacks as confirmation of Nostradamus's prophecies.

23. Bush's long-standing ties to leaders of the religious right (Pat Robertson, above all) help establish his bona fides. During the primary and general election campaign of 2000, Robertson and others held their followers solid for Bush, assuring them that he supported their values and would work for their cause once elected, even if he could not say so directly. In this fashion, they encouraged him to signal religious maximalists with winks, nudges, and coded allusions, while encouraging the faithful to listen for the same.

CHAPTER THREE

First presented as the plenary address of the American Academy of Religion, Rocky Mountain Regional meetings, Omaha, April 19, 2002.

1. Regarding *jihad*, see Rudolph Peters, *Jihad in Classical and Modern Islam* (Princeton: Markus Wiener, 1996); Reuven Firestone, *Jihad: The Origin of Holy War in Islam* (New York: Oxford University Press, 1999); Roxanne Euben, "The New Manichaeans," *Theory & Event* 5, no. 4 (2002), available at http://muse.jhu.edu/journals/theory_and_event/v005/5.4euben.html; and Roxanne Euben, "Killing (for) Politics: Jihad, Martyrdom and Political Action," *Political Theory* 30, no. 1 (February 2002): 4–35.

2. The wording of the two verses is identical.

> O Prophet, struggle [*jāhid*] with the unbelievers [*al-kuffār*] and hypocrites [*al-munāfiqīn*], and be thou harsh with them; their refuge is Gehenna—an evil homecoming.

Koran, trans. A. J. Arberry (New York: Touchstone, 1955), 1:216, 2:288. Note the classificatory intricacies of this passage, which hinge on the question of whether one is enjoined to wage the same kind of struggle (*jihad*) against both infidels and hypocrites. Aggressive war is unambiguously appropriate to the former, but if the latter are Muslims, this would be inappropriate. Instead, one should employ a form of peaceful, internal *jihad* aimed at (collective) self-perfection: moral criticism and religious injunction, perhaps. If this verse is taken to legitimate warfare against them, however, they have implicitly been classified as non-Muslim and alien to the collective self.

3. Koran, trans. Arberry, 1:94. See the remarks of Firestone, *Jihad*, pp. 78–79, on this passage.

4. Transcript of Pat Robertson's interview with Jerry Falwell, broadcast on the *700 Club*, September 13, 2001, available at www.pfaw.org/issues/right/robertson_falwell.html.

5. The most thoughtful and perceptive discussion of Falwell to date is that of Susan Harding, *The Book of Jerry Falwell: Fundamentalist Language and Politics* (Princeton: Princeton University Press, 2000). See also David Snowball, *Continuity and Change in the Rhetoric of the Moral Majority* (New York: Praeger, 1991); and Robert Boston, *Close Encounters with the Religious Right: Journeys into the Twilight Zone of Religion and Politics* (Amherst, N.Y.: Prometheus Press, 2000), pp. 105–22. The article on Falwell in J. Gordon Melton, Phillip Charles Lucas, and Jon R. Stone, *Prime-Time Religion: An Encyclopedia of Religious Broadcasting* (New York: Oryx Press, 1997), pp. 93–99, is thorough and useful.

6. "Falwell Apologizes to Gays, Feminists, Lesbians" (September 14, 2001), available at www.cnn.com/2001/US/09/14/Falwell.apology.index.html.

7. This support was particularly important in the crucial South Carolina primary, where Bush reestablished his front-runner status and beat back a serious challenge from John McCain. In the wake of that election, McCain excoriated both Robertson and Falwell, who happily returned his fire. See Mike Glover, "McCain Condemns Pat Robertson," *Washington Post*, February 28, 2000.

8. Laurie Goodstein, "Falwell: Blame Abortionists, Feminists and Gays," *New York Times*, September 14, 2001, available at www.guardian.co.uk/bush/story/0,7369,554232,00.html.

9. For immediate reactions, see Chris Kahn, "Robertson Defends Falwell," Associated Press September 16, 2001, available at www.amarillonet.com/stories/091601/ter_robertson.shtml; and Gustav Niebuhr, "U.S. 'Secular' Groups Set Tone for Terror Attacks, Falwell Says," *New York Times*, September 14, 2001, available at http://college3.nytimes.com/guests/articles/2001/

09/14/867953.xml. On Robertson, see the polemic works of Robert Boston, *The Most Dangerous Man in America? Pat Robertson and the Rise of the Christian Coalition* (Amherst, N.Y.: Prometheus Books, 1996); and Alec Foege, *The Empire God Built: Inside Pat Robertson's Media Machine* (New York: John Wiley, 1996); along with the article "Pat Robertson" in Melton et al., *Prime-Time Religion*, pp. 288–92.

10. "Falwell Apologizes to Gays, Feminists, Lesbians." The specification "I would never blame *any human being* . . . " apparently was meant to hold open the possibility that Falwell saw Satan's hand behind the events of September 11.

11. The verse Falwell meant to cite is Proverbs 14:34, which he properly supplied in subsequent press releases. That text reads: "Righteousness exalts a nation, but sin is a reproach to any people." The verse he cited to CNN is quite inappropriate and can only be regarded as a sort of biblical Freudian lapsus: "In all toil there is profit, but mere talk tends only to want." The error was corrected in subsequent Falwell releases, e.g., "Rev. Falwell's Statement, 'Why I Said What I Said,' 9/17/2001," available at www.justice-respect.org/bkg/falwell_statement_2001.html. It is also worth noting that Falwell made prominent use of Proverbs 14:34 in support of George W. Bush's primary campaign, as in his press release of March 23, 2000, entitled "Religious Right Gears Up for Battle," available at www.freerepublic.com/forum/a38dadf5256b0.htm.

12. "Falwell Apologizes to Gays, Feminists, Lesbians."

13. "Rev. Falwell's Statement, 'Why I Said What I Said,' 9/17/2001." This closely echoes the way in which Robertson presented his views on the *700 Club* broadcast, both for its form (first-person plural) and content:

> And we have thought that we're invulnerable. And we have been so concerned about money. We have been so concerned about material things. The interests of people are on their health and their finances, and on their pleasures and on their sexuality, and while this is going on while we're self-absorbed and the churches as well as in the population, we have allowed rampant pornography on the internet. We have allowed rampant secularism and occult, etc. to be broadcast on television. We have permitted somewhere in the neighborhood of 35 to 40 million unborn babies to be slaughtered in our society. We have a court that has essentially stuck its finger in God's eye and said we're going to legislate you out of the schools. We're going to take your commandments from off the courthouse steps in various states. We're not going to let little children read the commandments of God. We're not going to let the Bible be read, no prayer in our schools. We have insulted God at the highest levels of our government. And, then we say "why does this happen?" (§1)

14. Note Emile Benveniste's discussion of third-person pronouns as markers of those who are constituted as virtual nonpersons, excluded from conversation between "I" (or "we") and "you," in *Problems in General Linguistics* (Coral Gables: University of Miami Press, 1971), pp. 197–200.

15. Two different passages in Falwell's apology stand in contrast to one another and show these differing tendencies. The first makes clear his continuing view that certain specific people had created problems for all the nation, while conceding that he should not have identified them by name: "In retrospect, I should have mentioned the national sins without mentioning the organizations and persons by name." The second acknowledges that in addition to the sins of this first group—which he now calls "an unbelieving culture"—believers also shared some fault.

Their sins, however, were primarily sins of omission: "As I enumerated the sins of an unbeliev-ing culture, because of very limited time on the '700 Club,' I failed to point the finger at a sleep-ing, prayerless and carnal church. We believers must also acknowledge our sins, repent, and fast and pray for national revival" ("Rev. Falwell's Statement, 'Why I Said What I Said,' 9/17/2001").

16. "Falwell Apologizes for Remarks," *Washington Post*, September 18, 2001, p. C4.

17. Consider, for instance, the following passage from Robertson's 1990 book, *The New Mil-lennium*:

> Only by destroying the Christian consensus could this nation be undermined and its power destroyed. The assault against America has taken the following av-enues.
>
> First, the liberal left realized that no elected body in the United States would adopt its radical agenda. Therefore, a deliberate plan was put in motion to claim for non-elected judges power that they had never been given under the United States Constitution. Lawyers and judges would then, under the guise of "consti-tutional rights," dismantle systematically the Judeo-Christian majority consen-sus that has guided this nation since its founding.
>
> Second, and concurrently, the educational system would first be taken from its Christian roots and used as a psycho-political indoctrination ground to move the young toward the agenda of the left.
>
> Third, the left would infiltrate wealthy and powerful tax-free foundations and government agencies where taxpayers' funds would begin to pour out to sup-port the left at home and abroad.
>
> Fourth, organizations such as Planned Parenthood, the National Education Association, and more recently the National Organization for Women, People for the American Way, the Gay-Lesbian Caucus, and the ilk would arise to cham-pion unrestrained sex, homosexual rights, abortion on demand, while they attacked Christian beliefs, conservative organizations, and all the traditional family structures of America.
>
> Fifth, the nation's once conservative Christian press would be virtually over-whelmed by those dedicated to undermining Christian America in favor of this brave new world of humanism and socialism.

Pat Robertson, *The New Millennium* (1990), in *The Collected Works of Pat Robertson* (New York: In-spirational Press, 1994), pp. 148–49. Cf. Pat Robertson, *The Turning Tide* (Dallas: Word Pub-lishing, 1993), pp. 300–3. Further on Robertson's views, with particular attention to his shift from premillennialist apocalypticism to postmillennialist revivalism around the time of his 1988 presidential campaign, is Stephen O'Leary and Michael McFarland, "The Political Use of Mythic Discourse: Prophetic Interpretation in Pat Robertson's Presidential Campaign," *Quar-terly Journal of Speech* 75 (1989): 433–52.

18. "Rev. Falwell's Statement, 'Why I Said What I Said,' 9/17/2001."

19. Ibid. Regarding the deep background of this theme in American Protestantism, see John B. Boles, *The Great Revival: Beginnings of the Bible Belt* (Lexington: University Press of Kentucky, 1996); and William G. McLoughlin, *Revivals, Awakenings, and Reform: An Essay on Religion and Social Change in America, 1607–1977* (Chicago: University of Chicago Press, 1978).

20. For all that they collaborated on this and many other occasions, the two men have also been rivals for leadership of the religious right. During the 1980s Falwell was the more promi-

nent figure, but his star faded toward the end of that decade as Robertson's rose. The analogy of improvising musicians helps alert us to competition between the two performers, each trying to outdo the other.

21. Ibid.: "I was asking a Christian audience on a Christian TV program to claim II Chronicles 7:14 and repent." The same statement was made in the September 20 revision of this text, "Rev. Falwell's Statement, 'Why I Said What I Said.'"

22. Falwell's prominent use of this passage dates at least as far back as the beginning of his political activism. It is cited in the very first paragraph of his clarion text, *America Can Be Saved!* *(Jerry Falwell Preaches on Revival)* (Murfreesboro, Tenn.: Sword of the Lord Publishers, 1979), p. 7. To cite but a few relatively recent examples, see the following items among Falwell's many writings: "Mission Statement of the Thomas Road Baptist Church," available at www.falwell. com/mission.htm; "Changing the World One Life at a Time," sermon preached July 14, 1996, available at www.trbc.org/sermons/071496.html; "God's Plan to Save a Nation," sermon preached July 21, 1996, available at www.trbc.org/sermons/960721.html; "Bill Clinton Is Not America's Main Problem," sermon preached September 1998, available at www.trbc.org/sermons/980913v2.html; "Third Millennium Mysteries," sermon preached in 1999, available at www.trbc.org/sermons/990110.html; "America Deserves Bill Clinton," sermon preached in 1999, available at www.don-henley.com/main/amerdeserve.htm; and "A National Rebirth Needed," memo dated August 10, 2000, available at www.mcbible.com/Misc%20Data/Founding%20 Fathers.htm.

23. To give a faint idea of how popular this text is, a Google search of "II Chronicles 7:14" yielded more than eight thousand hits, the vast majority of which engaged the theme of revival. Regarding Reagan's use of the passage, see "Bibles and Scripture Passages Used by Presidents in Taking the Oath of Office," compiled by the Office of the Curator and Architect of the Capitol, available at http://memory.loc.gov/ammem/pihtml/pibible.html; on the 1980 "Washington for Jesus" rally, see Frederick Clarkson, *Eternal Hostility: The Struggle between Theocracy and Democracy* (Monroe, Me.: Common Courage Press, 1997), pp. 107–9; and Jeffrey Hadden and Anson Shupe, *Televangelism: Power and Politics on God's Frontier* (New York: Henry Holt, 1988), pp. 20–37; on the 1976 National Prayer Congress, see the summary of the archives for the event at the Billy Graham Center, available at www.wheaton.edu/bgc/archives/guides/176.htm.

24. Here it is probably worth noting that during the primary elections of 2000, Falwell formed an organization called People of Faith 2000, which solidly backed Bush and attacked all others, while cynically claiming it was not legally permitted to endorse candidates. The prime tasks he identified for this organization were (1) a call to prayer, based on II Chronicles 7:14; and (2) registry of 10 million new Christian voters (Jerry Falwell, "Calling Ten Million New Voters to Political Action," available at www.nljonline.com/April2000/April2.htm). See also the online discussion with Falwell organized by *USA Today* at the time of the Republican convention, "Conventions 2000: Rev. Jerry Falwell," *USA Today*, August 2, 2000, available at http://usatoday.com/community/chat/0802falwell.htm.

25. "Rev. Falwell's Statement, 'Why I Said What I Said,' 9/17/2001."

26. Jerry Falwell, "Why I Said What I Said," available at www.beliefnet.com/story/87/story_8781_2.html; my emphasis.

27. Jerry Falwell, "Pray for America," available at www.newsmax.com/archives/articles/2001/10/22/113353.shtml.

28. Jeff Zolony, "Bush Offers a Look into Spirituality," *Chicago Tribune*, January 7, 2002.

29. Ibid.; my emphasis. Perhaps coincidentally, but more likely not, a few weeks before

Bush's remarks, Karl Rove was quoted as saying that he and other political advisers to the president were concerned that religious conservatives were withdrawing from their participation in electoral politics. As a result, he and other Bush operatives intended to reach out to them with increased vigor. Jeff Zolony, "GOP Failed to Draw Religious Right in 2000, Says Bush Aide," *Chicago Tribune*, December 12, 2001.

30. Inter alia, see Sara Diamond, *Not by Politics Alone: The Enduring Influence of the Christian Right* (New York: Guilford Press, 1998); Melvin Urofsky and Martha May, eds., *The New Christian Right: Political and Social Issues* (New York: Garland, 1996); Duane Murray Oldfield, *The Right and the Righteous: The Christian Right Confronts the Republican Party* (Lanham, Md.: Rowman and Littlefield, 1996); and Michael Lienesch, *Redeeming America: Piety and Politics in the New Christian Right* (Chapel Hill: University of North Carolina Press, 1993). Much of the literature on the religious right is either alarmist or derisive. Glenn Utter and John Storey, *The Religious Right: A Reference Handbook* (Santa Barbara, Calif.: ABC-Clio, 1995), offers much useful information but is becoming dated.

31. Cf. Sayyid Qutb's observations about American clergy:

> The priest does not feel that his job is different from that of a stage manager or store manager. Success is first and prior to anything else. Means are unimportant; for success brings him good consequences: money and prestige. The greater the number of church-goers, the greater his income, prestige, and influence in the town.

Quoted in Ahmed Salah al-Din Mousalli, *Radical Islamic Fundamentalism: The Ideological and Political Discourse of Sayyid Qutb* (Beirut: American University of Beirut, 1992), pp. 27–28.

32. Several excellent studies of the *700 Club* have been published, although they reflect its nature in the 1980s and early '90s. Above all, see Janice Peck, *The Gods of Televangelism: The Crisis of Meaning and the Appeal of Religious Television* (Cresskill, N.J.: Hampton Press, 1993); and Stewart Hoover, *Mass Media Religion: The Social Sources of the Electronic Church* (Newbury Park, Calif.: Sage Publications, 1988). The figure of 7 million viewers is from Melton et al., *Prime-Time Religion*, p. 288. The most thorough analysis of audiences for religious television is the 1984 study carried out by the Annenberg School of Communications at the University of Pennsylvania for the National Religious Broadcasters Association: George Gerbner et al., *Religion and Television* (Philadelphia: Annenberg School of Communications, 1984). Based on this study, Peck describes the show's demographics as follows:

> [Within religious broadcasting,] [t]he "700 Club" . . . has the lowest number of viewers from rural areas and the fewest with only a grade-school education (29%). One quarter of the audience has some college education and 10% are graduates. The program attracts the largest proportion of viewers between 30 and 50 years old (47%), the highest share in the Midwest (40%), and the highest percentage of married viewers. It also has the greatest number of viewers who belong to and regularly attend a church. . . . [I]ts viewers are predominantly [*sic*] female in all age groups, and the Gallup study reported that more than 70% of its viewers over 50 years old are women. (p. 140)

On the difficulty of interpreting statistical evidence and the tendency of religious broadcasters to make wildly inflated claims, see Hadden and Shupe, *Televangelism*, pp. 143–59.

33. On several occasions the two men also used possessive pronouns to speak of the local congregations for which they held immediate pastoral responsibilities, as when Robertson told his guest, "I am thrilled to hear that about your church" (§17; cf. §§5, 15, 21). A certain slippage be-

tween these levels is evident in the first questions Robertson addressed to his guest: "What are you telling *the church*? You called *your church* together. What was your response at Thomas Road to this tragedy?" (§5; my emphasis).

34. These pronouns are very slippery, oscillating between the "we" that is the nation and the "we" that is the church. Insofar as the latter comes in for blame, it is primarily for sins of omission, as indicated by Robertson's verbs ("*We have allowed* rampant pornography on the internet. *We have allowed* rampant secularism and occult, etc. to be broadcast on television. *We have permitted* somewhere in the neighborhood of 35 to 40 million unborn babies to be slaughtered in our society" [§1; my emphasis]). Sins of commission, by contrast, are attributed to the non-church fraction of the nation, those more actively responsible for pornography, abortion, and the like.

35. The decisions of the "liberal" courts that are being referred to most often deal with the issues of abortion, school prayer, and separation of church and state. Although civil rights decisions beginning with *Brown v. Board of Education* (1954) are never explicitly mentioned, it is difficult to avoid the impression that they are subtextually present and very much at issue.

CHAPTER FOUR

First presented at Bates College, Department of German, Russian, and East Asian Languages & Literatures, fall 1997; subsequently at Dartmouth College, Department of Religious Studies; Reed College, Department of Religious Studies; and as a keynote address at "The Cultural Turn," conference organized by the University of California, Santa Barbara, Department of Sociology. An earlier version was published in Willi Braun and Russell T. McCutcheon, eds., *Guide to the Study of Religion* (London: Cassell Academic, 2000), pp. 409–22.

1. Here one should emphasize the importance of parental pride as a chief instrument of cultural reproduction. The satisfaction conveyed to a parent by the approbation of others is the chief payoff for the enormous labor it takes to produce properly socialized children, who can take their place as members of a group and ensure its continuity.

2. Judith Martin's observation in response to a gentleman who confessed himself disposed to employ a spoon where others more commonly use forks is apposite. "People who defy the simple customs of their own people arouse an amount of scorn that even Miss Manners finds surprising" (*Minneapolis Star Tribune*, September 11, 1996, p. E4).

3. I have discussed such processes more fully in *Discourse and the Construction of Society* (New York: Oxford University Press, 1989). Many other authors have pursued related issues, including Fredrik Barth, ed., *Ethnic Groups and Boundaries: The Social Organization of Culture Difference* (Boston: Little Brown, 1969); Erving Goffman, *Stigma: Notes on the Management of Spoiled Identity* (New York: Simon & Schuster, 1963); Basil Bernstein, *Class, Codes, and Control: Theoretical Studies towards a Sociology of Language* (New York: Schocken Books, 1975); Hans-Peter Hasenfratz, *Die Toten Lebenden: Eine Religionsphänomenologische Studie zum sozialen Tod in archaischen Gesellschaften* (Leiden: E. J. Brill, 1982); Norbert Elias, *The Civilizing Process*, 3 vols. (New York: Pantheon, 1983); Pierre Bourdieu, *Distinction: A Social Critique of the Judgment of Taste* (Cambridge: Harvard University Press, 1984); Dick Hebdige, *Subculture: The Meaning of Style* (London: Routledge, 1988); Michelle Lamont and Marcel Fournier, eds., *Cultivating Differences: Symbolic Boundaries and the Making of Inequality* (Chicago: University of Chicago Press, 1992); Norbert Elias and John L. Scotson, *The Established and the Outsiders* (New York: Sage Publications, 1994); and Raymond Williams, *Sociology of Culture* (Chicago: University of Chicago Press, 1995).

4. Here one perceives the etymological significance of Latin *cultura,* derived from the verb *colo,* "to cultivate, work the earth," as in *agri-cultura, horti-cultura,* etc. Transfer of this metaphor from the botanical to the human register implies a view of the person as a potential, like untilled soil, which demands the socializing labor of the collective if it is to bear fruit. Untended, it can remain fallow or grow wild into jungle.

5. The discourse of "values" has its strongest appeal for those concerned to normalize, naturalize, and stabilize that which I prefer to render problematic. The chief advantage in speaking of "preferences" rather than "values" is that it brings contingency and agency into the question.

6. Alternatively, one might take aesthetics to be concerned with questions regarding the things one encounters as sensuous objects; ethics, with those concerning encounters with other human (or at least animate) subjects.

7. That such strictures fall much more often and much more onerously on women reflects the patriarchal social structure of those who impose them, which gains force by being normalized as a sacred injunction.

8. Some measure of choice remains, albeit construed in the most prejudicial of terms. Religious regimes of orthopraxy thus offer the choice of accepting one's sacred duty or not. This entails further choices: to be a moral person and a proper member of the community or, alternatively, to become a rebel, heretic, and outsider in the eyes of others.

9. Voltaire, *Essai sur les moeurs,* chap. 121 (cf. chaps. 129, 187).

10. Of particular interest is Kant's 1784 definition of "Enlightenment" as "mankind's exit from its self-incurred immaturity," said immaturity being "the inability to make use of one's own understanding without the guidance of another," particularly in religious matters (Immanuel Kant, "An Answer to the Question: What Is Enlightenment" [1784], in *What Is Enlightenment: Eighteenth-Century Answers and Twentieth-Century Questions,* ed. James Schmidt [Berkeley: University of California Press, 1996], pp. 58–64).

11. Allen Wood, "The Enlightenment," in *Encyclopedia of Religion,* ed. M. Eliade (New York: Macmillan, 1987), 5:111. Publication of the *Encyclopédie* began in 1751 and was suspended in 1759, after the first seven volumes had appeared. The final ten volumes came out in 1765, after Diderot had obtained the king's tacit permission.

12. Here one should stress the marked difference of dress and comportment that separated Huguenots from Catholics in France or Catholic Cavaliers from Roundhead Puritans in England.

13. Official responses to Kant's text give an indication of the extent to which his position was not only innovative, but profoundly challenging to an older regime of truth. Under policies instituted with the accession of Friedrich Wilhelm II to the Prussian throne in 1786, Kant submitted his manuscript to be vetted for publication by officials of the state department of church and schools. Book 1 of his text was cleared in 1791 and published in the *Berlinische Monatsschrift* of April 1792. Book 2, however, was rejected on the ground that it controverted biblical teachings. Kant then took books 2–4 to the philosophical faculty at the University of Jena and received their imprimatur, after which he published the full text in 1793. One year later (October 1794), he received the following communication from the king himself:

> Our most high person has for a long time observed with great displeasure how you misuse your philosophy to undermine and debase many of the most important and fundamental doctrines of the Holy Scriptures and Christianity; how, namely, you have done this in your book, *Religion within the Limits of Reason Alone,* as well as in other smaller works. . . . We demand of you immediately a

most conscientious answer and expect that in the future, towards the avoidance
of our highest disfavor, you will give no such cause for offense, but rather, in ac-
cordance with your duty, employ your talents and authority so that our paternal
purpose may be more and more attained. If you continue to resist, you may cer-
tainly expect unpleasant consequences to yourself.

Trans. Theodore M. Green, "The Historical Context and Religious Significance of Kant's *Religion*," introduction to Immanuel Kant, *Religion within the Limits of Reason Alone* (New York:
Harper and Row, 1960), p. xxxiv. Kant was forced to submit and wrote to the king that thereafter
he would "entirely refrain from all public statements on religion, both natural and revealed, either in lectures or writings," a promise he abandoned with Friedrich Wilhelm's death in 1797.

14. Particularly noteworthy is the way the discourse of genius and inspiration is secularized
in the eighteenth and nineteenth centuries, constructing a form of intellectual/artistic authority
that largely supplants authority based on claims of divine revelation.

15. Sociologists and others have often perceived the question of "secularization" as one of
church attendance, which makes it easy to quantify but also misconstrues it badly. The issue is
not just what proportion of a population retains membership in religious institutions and how
faithfully they attend religious services. Of much greater importance—and much more difficult
to measure—are such questions as the extent to which religious discourse penetrates other cultural domains; the number of practices organized in accord with explicitly religious precepts; the
extent to which persons experience their identity in specifically religious terms; the extent to
which the community submits to the control of religious institutions; and so forth.

16. There are probably many reasons for this fact, but two seem particularly important. First,
in contrast to religious institutions, philosophy remained very much the pursuit of an intellectual elite and developed no effective channels or instruments for the diffusion of its results to
popular audiences. Second, as an explicitly human discourse, philosophy did not claim the same
level of authority as did religion and could not command the same respectful obeisance. Representing one's results as "conclusions reached by very smart people after a lot of deep thought" is
nowhere near so effective as representing them as "God's word." Should its adherents come to
regard a philosophical system as a firm, foundational truth that may be interpreted but not in-
terrogated (some varieties of Marxism or psychoanalysis, for example), it begins to function
more as a religion than a philosophy. This shift may also be reflected in a hardening of institutional structures that serve to propagate the doctrine, regulate credentials, organize practice, and
enforce orthodoxy.

17. Sayyid Qutb, *Milestones*, trans. Ahmad Zaki Hammad (Indianapolis: American Trust
Publications, 1990). Arabic original, *Ma'alim fi al-tariq* (1964).

CHAPTER FIVE

First presented at Mount St. Mary's College, Department of Theology, fall 1997; subsequently at
Århus University, Institute for the Study of Religion. An earlier version was published in Mark
Taylor, ed., *Critical Terms for Religious Studies* (Chicago: University of Chicago Press, 1998),
pp. 55–69.

1. The literature on nationalism is enormous and constantly growing. Benedict Anderson's
Imagined Communities: Reflections on the Origin and Spread of Nationalism (London: Verso, 1983),
has long been the most influential single item, but many others bear consultation, including E.

J. Hobsbawm, *Nations and Nationalism Since 1780* (Cambridge: Cambridge University Press, 1990); Partha Chatterjee, *The Nation and Its Fragments* (Princeton: Princeton University Press, 1993); Josep Llobera, *The God of Modernity: The Development of Nationalism in Western Europe* (Oxford: Berg, 1994); Geoffrey Hosking and George Schöpflin, eds., *Myths and Nationhood* (London: Routledge, 1997); R. D. Grillo, *Pluralism and the Politics of Difference: State, Culture, and Ethnicity in Comparative Perspective* (Oxford: Clarendon Press, 1998); Peter van der Veer and Hartmut Lehmann, eds., *Nation and Religion: Perspectives on Europe and Asia* (Princeton: Princeton University Press, 1999); and Anthony D. Smith, *Myths and Memories of the Nation* (Oxford: Oxford University Press, 1999). The materials collected in Geoff Eley and Ronald Suny, eds., *Becoming National: A Reader* (New York: Oxford University Press, 1996), make for a good entrée into the subject.

2. The usually forgotten subtitle of Hobbes's masterwork holds particular interest for its care to separate religious concerns from those that will become proper to a more secular state: *Leviathan, or the Matter, Form, and Power of a Commonwealth, Ecclesiastical and Civil* (1651).

3. To be sure, there were earlier foundations on which modern nationalism built, but the role of the people (or "folk") in such formations was quite different, as was the relation of nation to state and church alike. On these antecedents, see Colette Beaune, *The Birth of an Ideology: Myths and Symbols of Nation in Late-Medieval France*, trans. Susan Huston (Berkeley: University of California Press, 1991); Adrian Hastings, *The Construction of Nationhood: Ethnicity, Religion, and Nationalism* (Cambridge: Cambridge University Press, 1997); and David Bell, *The Cult of the Nation in France: Inventing Nationalism 1680–1800* (Cambridge: Harvard University Press, 2001).

4. On military mobilization, the classic work is Richard Cobb, *The People's Armies*, trans. Marianne Elliott (New Haven: Yale University Press, 1987); on the festivals, see Mona Ozouf, *Festivals and the French Revolution*, trans. Alan Sheridan (Cambridge: Harvard University Press, 1988).

5. The crucial text of this period is Johann Gottlieb Fichte, *Addresses to the German Nation*, trans. R. F. Jones and G. H. Turnbull (Chicago: Open Court, 1922), on which see Martin Thom, *Republics, Nations, and Tribes* (London: Verso, 1995).

6. The classic statement of nationalist ideology, Ernest Renan's "What Is a Nation?"—readily available in Eley and Suny, *Becoming National*, pp. 42–55—derives from this precise context and should always be read with reference to it. More broadly on the construction of nation and citizens in the Third Republic, see Eugen Weber, *Peasants into Frenchman: The Modernization of Rural France, 1870–1914* (Stanford: Stanford University Press, 1976); and Mona Ozouf, *L'École, l'Église et la République, 1871–1914* (Paris: A. Colin, 1963).

7. Émile Durkheim, *Elementary Forms of the Religious Life*, trans. Karen Fields (New York: Free Press, 1995; French original, 1912). From a more conventionally religious perspective, one might also describe the cult of the nation as a form of idolatry or fetishism.

8. On the Iranian Revolution, see Michael M. J. Fischer, *Iran: From Religious Dispute to Revolution* (Cambridge: Harvard University Press, 1980); M. M. Salehi, *Insurgency through Culture and Religion: The Islamic Revolution of Iran* (New York: Praeger, 1988); Mansoor Moaddel, *Class, Politics, and Ideology in the Iranian Revolution* (New York: Columbia University Press, 1993); Hamid Dabashi, *Theology of Discontent: The Ideological Foundations of the Islamic Revolution in Iran* (New York: New York University Press, 1993); Haggay Ram, *Myth and Mobilization in Revolutionary Iran: The Use of the Friday Congregational Sermon* (Washington: American University Press, 1994); Annabelle Sreberny-Mohammadi and Ali Mohammadi, *Small Media, Big Revolu-*

tion: Communication, Culture, and the Iranian Revolution (Minneapolis: University of Minnesota Press, 1994); and Akbar Molajani, *Sociologie politique de la révolution iranienne de 1979* (Paris: Harmattan, 1999).

9. On the Muslim Brotherhood, see Gilles Kepel, *Muslim Extremism in Egypt: The Prophet and Pharaoh*, trans. Jon Rothschild (Berkeley: University of California Press, 1985); Johannes J. G. Jansen, *The Neglected Duty: The Creed of Sadat's Assassins and Islamic Resurgence in the Middle East* (New York: Macmillan, 1986); on the Taliban, see Ahmed Rashid, *Taliban: Militant Islam, Oil, and Fundamentalism in Central Asia* (New Haven: Yale University Press, 2000); on religious parties in Israel, see Ehud Sprinzak, *The Ascendance of Israel's Radical Right* (New York: Oxford University Press, 1991); and Aviezer Ravitzky, *Messianism, Zionism, and Jewish Religious Radicalism*, trans. Michael Swirsky and Jonathan Chipman (Chicago: University of Chicago Press, 1996); on the Spanish civil war, see Gerald Brenan, *The Spanish Labyrinth: An Account of the Social and Political Background of the Civil War* (Cambridge: Cambridge University Press, 1967); and José M. Sánchez, *The Spanish Civil War as a Religious Tragedy* (Notre Dame: University of Notre Dame Press, 1987).

10. On Sri Lanka, see Bruce Kapferer, *Legends of People, Myths of State: Violence, Intolerance, and Political Culture in Sri Lanka and Australia* (Washington: Smithsonian Institution Press, 1988); Stanley J. Tambiah, *Buddhism Betrayed? Religion, Politics, and Violence in Sri Lanka* (Chicago: University of Chicago Press, 1992), and *Leveling Crowds: Ethnonationalist Conflicts and Collective Violence in South Asia* (Berkeley: University of California Press, 1996); on the Sudan, Ann Mosely Lesch, *The Sudan: Contested National Identities* (Bloomington: Indiana University Press, 1998); and Jay Spaulding and Stephanie Beswick, eds., *White Nile, Black Blood: War, Leadership, and Ethnicity from Khartoum to Kampala* (Lawrenceville, N.J.: Red Sea Press, 2000), mark a good beginning.

11. See Peter van der Veer, *Religious Nationalism: Hindus and Muslims in India* (Berkeley: University of California Press, 1994); Lise McKean, *Divine Enterprise: Gurus and the Hindu Nationalist Movement* (Chicago: University of Chicago Press, 1996); Thomas Hansen, *The Saffron Wave: Democracy and Hindu Nationalism in Modern India* (Princeton: Princeton University Press, 1999).

12. On the Balkan struggles, see Sabrina Ramet, *Balkan Babel: Politics, Religion, and Culture in Yugoslavia* (Boulder: Westview Press 1992); Tone Bringa, *Being Muslim the Bosnian Way: Identity and Community in a Central Bosnian Village* (Princeton: Princeton University Press, 1995); Michael A. Sells, *The Bridge Betrayed: Religion and Genocide in Bosnia* (Berkeley: University of California Press, 1996); G. Scott Davis, ed., *Religion and Justice in the War Over Bosnia* (New York: Routledge, 1996); Paul Mojzes, ed., *Religion and the War in Bosnia* (Atlanta: Scholars Press, 1998).

13. On Northern Ireland, see John Fulton, *The Tragedy of Belief: Religion, Division, and Politics in Ireland* (New York: Oxford University Press 1991); Lucy Bryson and Clem McCartney, eds., *Clashing Symbols: A Report on the Use of Flags, Anthems, and Other National Symbols in Northern Ireland* (Belfast: Institute of Irish Studies, 1994); Seamus Dunn, *Facets of the Conflict in Northern Ireland* (New York: St. Martin's Press, 1995); Anthony Buckley, *Negotiating Identity: Rhetoric, Metaphor, and Social Drama in Northern Ireland* (Washington, D.C.: Smithsonian Institution Press, 1995); Joseph Ruane and Jennifer Todd, *The Dynamics of Conflict in Northern Ireland* (Cambridge: Cambridge University Press, 1996); Anthony Buckley, ed., *Symbols in Northern Ireland* (Belfast: Institute of Irish Studies, 1998); and Dominic Bryan, *Orange Parades: The Politics of Ritual, Tradition and Control* (London: Pluto Press, 2000).

14. Struggles over territory that one or both parties constitute as holy are often among the most bitter and intractable, sacred space being among the world's scarcest and most precious resources. Compare, for instance, the situation of Israelis and Palestinians regarding Jerusalem, on which see Richard Hecht and Roger Friedland, *To Rule Jerusalem* (New York: Cambridge University Press, 1996). Compare also the campaign Hindu nationalists waged to clear the Babri Masjid Mosque from Ayodhya, or the indomitable efforts of the Lakota to recover the Black Hills.

15. Prior to the Enlightenment, it was not unusual for Europeans to organize for lethal violence on behalf of their religious community, as the Crusades and Wars of Religion make patently clear. In subsequent centuries politics, society, and culture were revised in the West such that only the state could undertake such bloody projects with any claim of legitimacy. When ad hoc groups attempt to do so, we are conditioned to regard them as gangsters, pirates, terrorists, and the like. When they do so in the name of religion, the term we employ is "fanatics." The al Qaeda perspective is quite the reverse, positing religion as the only possible entity on behalf of which armed struggle is legitimate. The proposition is arguable but strikes us as perverse, or at least medieval.

16. Here it is worth noting that in early November 2001, bin Laden raised the level of his rhetoric against the heads of Muslim states whom he had previously denounced as "hypocrites." Angered that they had not rallied to his earlier calls for Islamic solidarity, he seems to have traced this failure to their entanglement in international relations among states as mediated through the United Nations. "Those who want to solve our tragedies through the U.N. are hypocrites, deceiving God, the prophet and deceiving all believers. Who issued the resolution on the division of Palestine in 1947 which gave the Muslim country to the Jews? It was the U.N. Those who pretend they are leaders of the Arab world and remain members of the U.N. are infidels" (Neil MacFarquhar and Jim Rutenberg, "Bin Laden, in a Taped Speech, Says Attacks in Afghanistan Are a War against Islam," *New York Times,* 4 November 2001, p. B2). Since one wages *jihad* against infidels, but not against fellow Muslims ("hypocrites" included), this exercise in reclassification carries a serious implicit threat.

CHAPTER SIX

Initially presented as keynote to a conference on "Religion and Revolution" organized by the University of Minnesota, Religious Studies Program, November 8, 1981. Published in Bruce Lincoln, ed., *Religion, Rebellion, Revolution* (London: Macmillan, 1985), pp. 266–92.

1. I have in mind here purely philosophical or theological interpretations of religion, as well as the structuralist school of cultural anthropology.

2. For the École sociologique, see Émile Durkheim, *The Elementary Forms of the Religious Life,* trans. J. W. Swain (London: George Allen & Unwin, 1915); and the pieces collected in Marcel Mauss, *Oeuvres, 1. Les Fonctions sociales du sacré,* ed. Victor Karady (Paris: Minuit, 1968). For the functionalists, see Bronislaw Malinowski, *Magic, Science and Religion and Other Essays* (Garden City, N.J.: Doubleday, 1954); and A. R. Radcliffe-Brown, *Structure and Function in Primitive Society* (New York: Free Press, 1965), esp. pp. 153–77. For the Chicago school, see Mircea Eliade, *The Myth of the Eternal Return* (Princeton: Princeton University Press, 1954), and *The Sacred and the Profane* (New York: Harcourt Brace Jovanovich, 1959).

3. The most important works of Marx and Engels dealing with religion have been conveniently collected in *Marx and Engels on Religion* (New York: Schocken, 1967). The best secondary works on Marx's analysis to date are Charles Wackenheim, *La Failité de la religion d'après Karl*

Marx (Paris: PUF, 1963); and Werner Post, *Kritik der Religion bei Karl Marx* (Munich: Kösel, 1969). Engels's differences with Marx come out most clearly in *The Peasant War in Germany* and "On the History of Early Christianity," and have been discussed by Marcello Fedele, "Marxismo e critica dell' ideologica religiosa. Una reinterpretazione," introduction to Marx and Engels, *Scritti sulla religione* (Rome: Giulio Savelli, 1973), pp. 7–43, which Cristiano Grottanelli was good enough to call to my attention. For the Manchester school, see Max Gluckman, *Order and Rebellion in Tribal Africa* (New York: Free Press, 1963), esp. pp. 110–36, and *Essays on the Ritual of Social Relations* (Manchester: University of Manchester Press, 1962), pp. 1–52. Among the works of Barthes, I have in mind primarily his *Mythologies*, translated by A. Lavers (London: Jonathan Cape, 1972), pp. 109–59.

4. Vittorio Lanternari, *The Religions of the Oppressed*, trans. L. Sergio (New York: Alfred A. Knopf, 1963).

5. Wilhelm Mühlmann, *Chiliasmus und Nativismus* (Berlin: Dietrich Reimer, 1961); Peter Worsley, *The Trumpet Shall Sound*, 2nd ed. (New York: Schocken, 1968); and Kenelm Burridge, *New Heaven, New Earth* (New York: Schocken, 1969); see also Anthony F. C. Wallace, "Revitalization Movements," *American Anthropologist* 58 (1956): 264–81; Yonina Talmon, "Pursuit of the Millennium: The Relation between Religious and Social Change," *Archives europénes de sociologie* 3 (1962): 125–48; and Bryan Wilson, *Magic and the Millennium* (Frogmore, St. Albans: Paladin, 1975).

6. E. M. Hobsbawm, *Primitive Rebels* (Manchester: Manchester University Press, 1959), esp. pp. 57–107; Norman Cohn, *Pursuit of the Millennium*, rev. ed. (New York: Oxford University Press, 1970); Bernard Töpfer, *Das kommende Reich des friedens* (Berlin: Dietrich Reimer, 1964); and Gerschon Scholem, *Sabbatai Sevi, the Mystical Messiah* (Princeton: Princeton University Press, 1973).

7. Christopher Hill, *Puritanism and Revolution* (London: Secker and Warburg, 1958), esp. pp. 57–107, and *The World Turned Upside Down* (New York: Viking, 1972); Michael Walzer, *Revolution of the Saints* (Cambridge: Harvard University Press, 1965); Christopher Dawson, *The Gods of Revolution* (New York: Minerva, 1975); and Michel Vovelle, *Religion et révolution: La Déchristianisation de l'an II* (Paris: Hachette, 1976).

8. On Chinese movements prior to significant European influence, see Werner Eichhorn, "Description of the Rebellion of Sun En and Earlier Taoist Rebellions," *Mitteilungen des Instituts für Orientforschung* 2 (1954): 325–52; Vincent Y. C. Shih, "Some Chinese Rebel Ideologies," *T'oung pao* 44 (1956): 150–226; Yuji Muramatsu, "Some Themes in Chinese Rebel Ideologies," in *The Confucian Persuasion*, ed. A. F. Wright (Stanford: Stanford University Press, 1960), pp. 241–67; Kao Yu-kung, "A Study of the Fang La Rebellion," *Harvard Journal of Asiatic Studies* 24 (1962): 17–63; Anna K. Seidel, "The Image of the Perfect Ruler in Early Taoist Messianism," *History of Religions* 9 (1969): 216–47; G. H. Dunstheimer, "Quelques aspects religieux des sociétés secrètes," *Mouvements populaires et sociétés secrètes en chine aux XIXᵉ et XXᵉ siècles* (Paris: Maspero, 1970), pp. 65–73; Susan Naquin, *Millenarian Rebellion in China* (New Haven: Yale University Press, 1976); and Frederick Wakeman, "Rebellion and Revolution: The Study of Popular Movements in Chinese History," *Journal of Asian Studies* 36 (1977): 201–38.

On the Kharijites, see Elie Abid Salem, *Political Theory and Institutions of the Khawārij* (Baltimore: Johns Hopkins University Press, 1956); and G. Levi della Vida, "Khārijites," in *Encyclopedia of Islam*, vol. 4 (Leiden: E. J. Brill, 1978), pp. 1074–77.

There is still no truly adequate treatment of the Mahdist insurrection in the Sudan, but one should note Alan Buchan Theobald, *The Mahdiya*, 2nd ed. (London: Longmans, 1967); Peter M. Holt, *The Mahdist State in the Sudan*, 2nd ed. (Oxford: Oxford University Press, 1970); L. Carl Brown, "The Sudanese Mahdia," in *Protest and Power in Black Africa*, ed. Robert Rotberg and Ali Mazrui (New York: Oxford University Press, 1970); and R. H. Dekmejian and M. J. Wyszominski, "Charismatic Leadership in Islam: The Mahdi of the Sudan," *Comparative Studies in Society and History* 14 (1972): 193–214.

On the Nizaris, Marshall G. S. Hodgson's *The Order of Assassins* (The Hauge: Mouton, 1955) remains the standard work. Also of value are Rudolf Gelpke, "Der Geheimbund von Alamut— Legende und Wirklichkeit," *Antaios* 8 (September 1966): 269–93; and Bernard Lewis, *The Assassins* (London: Weidenfeld and Nicolson, 1967).

On the Iranian Revolution, see Michael M. J. Fischer, *Iran: From Religious Dispute to Revolution* (Cambridge: Harvard University Press, 1980); Kurt Greussing and Jan Heren Grevemeyer, eds. *Revolution in Iran und Afghanistan* (Frankfurt: Syndikat, 1980); Jerrold D. Green, *Revolution in Iran: The Politics of Countermobilization* (New York: Praeger, 1982); and Mary Hegland, "Two Images of Husain: Accommodation and Revolution in an Iranian Village," in *Religion and Politics in Iran*, ed. Nikki R. Keddie (New Haven: Yale University Press, 1983), pp. 218–35. Valuable background information is to be found in Shahrough Akhavi, *Religion and Politics in Contemporary Iran: Clergy-State Relations in the Pahlavi Period* (Albany: State University of New York Press, 1980); Aram Katouzian, *The Political Economy of Modern Iran* (New York: New York University Press, 1981); and Nikki R. Keddie, *Roots of Revolution: An Interpretive History of Modern Iran* (New Haven: Yale University Press, 1981).

9. George Rudé, *Ideology and Popular Protest* (New York: Pantheon, 1980), esp. pp. 13–38. Rudé's study is particularly valuable for his extension of Marx's notion of ideology to classes other than the bourgeoisie (following Gramsci) and his view of how "inherent" and "derived" ideas coalesce in the formation of popular ideologies.

10. To my mind, one of the most difficult of all questions is assessing the extent to which "secular" ideologies of the nineteenth and twentieth centuries—Marxism, anarchism, psychoanalysis, and the like—are significantly different from religious ideologies, and to what extent the undeniable differences between these two modes of ideology are more superficial than substantive. What can be observed is that until relatively recently in human history, all ideologies were explicitly religious. Within the last two centuries, however, such developments as the emergence of the modern nation-state, mass communications, and industrial production have created a situation in which ostensibly nonreligious ideologies have come into being and flourish alongside of religious ideologies. One most note, however, that these new ideologies still possess powerful mythic, ritual, and soteriological dimensions, whatever their position toward "religion" per se. At the very least, we may thus be justified in calling them "para-religious."

11. Insofar as the excess wealth controlled by the dominant fraction is derived from other segments of society whose interests are not served by the religion of the status quo, the professionals of that religion can ultimately be seen as parasitic on those segments. It is, however, a parasitism at secondhand, being mediated by the parasitism of the dominant fraction.

12. In the discussion of the Confucian literati, I have followed Etienne Balázs, *Chinese Civilization and Bureaucracy*, trans. H. M. Wright (New Haven: Yale University Press, 1964), esp. pp. 13–27, 150–70; T'ung-tsu Ch'ü, "Chinese Class Structure and Its Ideology," in *Chinese Thought and Institutions*, ed. J. K. Fairbank (Chicago: University of Chicago Press, 1957), pp. 235–50; and C. K. Yang, *Religion in Chinese Society* (Berkeley: University of California Press, 1961).

13. Balázs, *Chinese Civilization and Bureaucracy*, p. 18.

14. T'ung-tsu Ch'ü, "Chinese Class Structure and Its Ideology," p. 237, citing the Confucian sage of the Chou dynasty, Hsün-tzu.

15. The ideology of the Mandate of Heaven is extremely interesting, in that it legitimates not only any current ruler, but also the fall of any ruler and advent of a new one, even a rebel or usurper, such events being described as the withdrawal and rebestowal of heavenly favor. The position of the literati, however, is not affected by such shifts, and the literati have invariably been able to reassert their control of society and the state after every dynastic shift in Chinese history, including that of 1949. While Confucian ideology thus allows for changes in political rule, it continues to serve the interests of the dominant social fraction.

16. Here I have largely followed Christopher Hill, *The Century of Revolution* (Edinburgh: Thomas Nelson, 1961), and *The World Turned Upside Down;* and William M. Lamont, *Godly Rule: Politics and Religion 1603–1660* (New York: St. Martin's, 1969).

17. See the discussion in Michael Walzer, *Regicide and Revolution* (Cambridge: Cambridge University Press, 1974), pp. 12–13, 21–27, et passim, following E. Kantorowicz, *The King's Two Bodies* (Princeton: Princeton University Press, 1957).

18. Hill, *Century of Revolution*, p. 77.

19. The great exception (which appeared after original publication of this chapter and transformed study in this area) is Jean and John Comaroff, *Of Revelation and Revolution: Christianity, Colonialism, and Consciousness in South Africa*, 2 vols. (Chicago: University of Chicago Press, 1991–95). See also Peter Lawrence, *Road Belong Cargo* (Manchester: Manchester University Press, 1964), passim; and Robert Tonkison, *The Jigalong Mob* (Menlo Park, Calif.: Cummings, 1974), esp. pp. 117–33.

20. A major point of debate regarding millenarian movements is the extent to which they may be considered as movements of lower-class social protest. Norman Cohn—in *Pursuit of the Millennium*, pp. 281–86, and "Medieval Millenarism: Its Bearing on the Comparative Study of Millennarian Movements," in *Millennial Dreams in Action*, ed. S. Thrupp (The Hague: Mouton, 1962), pp. 31–43—has tended to reject such a view, as has Michael Adas, *Prophets of Rebellion* (Chapel Hill: University of North Carolina Press, 1979), pp. 184ff., while such authors as Lanternari, *Religions of the Oppressed;* Worsley, *Trumpet Shall Sound*, pp. xxxix–xvii, 225–27; and Talmon, "Pursuit of the Millennium," pp. 136–38, have taken the opposite view.

21. That such groups of necessity constitute a threat to the religion of the status quo and the dominant social fraction was already recognized by Wallace, "Revitalization Movements," p. 274; Lanternari, *Religions of the Oppressed*, p. 43; and Worsley, *Trumpet Shall Sound*, p. xxxvii. On the existence of alternative ideologies within society and the challenge they pose to the established order, see Rudé, *Ideology and Popular Protest*, and the extremely interesting treatment of W. F. Wertheim, "La Société et les conflits entre systèmes de valeurs," *Cahiers internationaux de sociologie* 28 (1960): 33–46.

To pursue the examples cited above, note the strong resistance to religious toleration within Stuart England and the repeated persecutions of heterodox sects in traditional China. On the latter, see the classic (but dated) work of J. J. M. DeGroot, *Sectarianism and Religious Persecution in China* (Amsterdam: Johannes Müller, 1903).

22. Among the many excellent studies of such groups, see Bengt Sundkler, *Bantu Prophets in South Africa*, 2nd ed. (London: Oxford University Press, 1961); Georges Balandier, "Messianismes et nationalismes en Afrique Noir," *Cahiers internationaux de sociologie* 14 (1953): 41–64; David F. Aberle, *The Peyote Religion among the Navaho* (Chicago: Viking Fund Publications in An-

thropology, 1966); Joseph Jorgensen, *The Sun Dance Religion* (Chicago: University of Chicago Press, 1972); Roger Bastide, *The African Religions of Brazil*, trans. H. Sebba (Baltimore: Johns Hopkins University Press, 1978); and Al Raboteau, *Slave Religion* (New York: Oxford University Press, 1978). Regrettably, there is still no adequate treatment of the Rastafarians.

23. Balázs, *Chinese Civilization and Bureaucracy*, p. 17.

24. Hodgson, *Order of Assassins*, pp. 6, 41; Lewis, *The Assassins*, pp. 20ff.

25. Jorgensen, *Sun Dance Religion*, esp. pp. 231ff.

26. On the Wahhabis, see Lansiné Kaba, *The Wahhābīya* (Evanston, Ill.: Northwestern University Press, 1974). On the Sanusi, see E. E. Evans-Pritchard, *The Sanusi of Cyrenaica* (Oxford: Clarendon Press, 1949); and Nicola A. Ziadeh, *Sanūsīyah: A Study of a Revivalist Movement in Islam* (Leiden: E. J. Brill, 1958). On the Brotherhood of the Free Spirit, see Cohn, *Pursuit of the Millennium*, pp. 148–86; and Robert E. Lerner, *The Heresy of the Free Spirit in the Later Middle Ages* (Berkeley: University of California Press, 1972). On the Seven Sages of the Bamboo Grove, see Balázs, *Chinese Civilization and Bureaucracy*, pp. 236–42.

27. Jean Baechler, *Revolution*, trans. J. Vickers (New York: Harper and Row, 1975), pp. 189ff.

28. Muramatsu, "Some Themes in Chinese Rebel Ideologies," p. 255.

29. Thus, e.g., Adas, *Prophets of Rebellion*, pp. 284ff.; and Burridge, *New Heaven, New Earth*, pp. 153–63.

30. Worsley, *Trumpet Shall Sound*, pp. ix–xviii.

31. See Hill, *World Turned Upside Down*, pp. 187, 198ff.

32. Adas, *Prophets of Rebellion*, p. 187.

33. For a discussion of the formation of the Kikuyu African Orthodox Church and the Kikuyu Pentecostal Church and the controversy with European missions over clitoridectomy, see L. S. B. Leakey, "The Kikuyu Problems of the Initiation of Girls," *Journal of the Royal Anthropological Institute* 61 (1931): 277–85; Ralph Bunche, "The Irua Ceremony among the Kikuyu," *Journal of Negro History* 26 (1941): 46–65; Mühlmann, *Chiliasmus und Nativismus*, pp. 118–21; Jomo Kenyatta, *Facing Mount Kenya* (New York: Vintage, 1965), pp. 125–48; and Carl G. Rosberg Jr. and John Nottingham, *The Myth of 'Mau Mau': Nationalism in Kenya* (Stanford: Hoover Institution Press, 1966), pp. 105–35.

34. For knowledgeable and sympathetic assessments of the Mau Mau, one should ignore the writings of L. S. B. Leakey and see, rather, Mühlmann, *Chiliasmus und Nativismus*, pp. 105–40; Rosberg and Nottingham, *Myth of 'Mau Mau'*; Vickie Cauché, "Kenya: Les Origines de la crise," *Cahiers internationaux* 41 (1952), pp. 82–90; George Padmore, "Behind the Mau Mau," *Phylon* 14 (1953): 355–72, Martin L. Kilson Jr., "Behind the Mau Mau Rebellion," *Dissent* 3 (1963): 264–75; Gilbert Kushner, "An African Revitalization Movement: Mau Mau," *Anthropos* 60 (1965): 763–802; and, most especially, Robert Buijtenhuijs, *Le Mouvement 'Mau-Mau'* (The Hague: Mouton, 1971).

The importance of the land issue has been stressed by all of the above, and separately treated by Ralph Bunche, "The Land Equation in Kenya Colony," *Journal of Negro History* 24 (1939): 33–43; and Martin L. Kilson Jr., "Land and the Kikuyu," *Journal of Negro History* 40 (1955): 103–53. The most eloquent testimony, however, remains that of Kenyatta:

> In studying the Gikuyu tribal organisation it is necessary to take into consideration land tenure as the most important factor in the social, political, religious, and economic life of the tribe. As agriculturalists, the Gikuyu people depend entirely on the land. It supplies them with the material needs of life, through which spiritual and mental contentment is achieved. Communion with the an-

cestral spirits is perpetuated through contact with the soil in which the ancestors of the tribe lie buried. The Gikuyu consider the earth as the "mother" of the
tribe, for the reason that the mother bears her burden about eight or nine
months while the child is in her womb, and then for a short period of suckling.
But it is the soil that feeds the child through lifetime, and again after death it is
the soil that nurses the spirits of the dead for eternity. (*Facing Mount Kenya*,
p. 22)

35. Hill, *Century of Revolution*, p. 13.

36. Some of the more important literature on millenarianism is listed above in notes 5 and
6, to which should be added Efraim Andersson, *Messianic Popular Movements in the Lower Congo*,
trans. D. Burton (Uppsala: Almquist and Wiksells, 1958); Kenelm O. L. Burridge, *Mambu: A
Melanesian Millennium* (New York: Humanities Press, 1960); Lawrence, *Road Belong Cargo*; I. C.
Jarvie, *The Revolution in Anthropology* (London: Routledge & Kegan Paul, 1964); the essays in
Sylvia Thrupp, ed., *Millennial Dreams in Action* (The Hague: Mouton, 1962), and those in volumes 4 and 5 of the *Archives de sociologie des religions* (1957–58), entitled "Messianismes et mil-
lenarismes" and "Les Messianismess dans le monde," respectively.

For the role of millennial thought within the English civil war and the French Revolution, see
B. S. Capp, *The Fifth Monarchy Men* (London: Faber & Faber, 1972); Paul Christianson, *Reformers
and Babylon: English Apocalyptic Visions from the Reformation to the Eve of the Civil War* (Toronto:
University of Toronto Press, 1970); and the extremely interesting study of Clarke Garrett, *Re-
spectable Folly: Millenarians and the French Revolution in France and England* (Baltimore: Johns
Hopkins University Press, 1975).

37. See Bruce Lincoln, "Der politische Gehalt des Mythos," in *Alcheringa: Studien zu Mytho-
logie, Schamanismus, und Religion*, ed. Hans-Peter Duerr (Frankfurt: Qumran, 1983), pp. 9–25;
Talmon, "Pursuit of the Millennium," esp. pp. 130–32, has argued along similar lines.

38. Historians have long debated whether the ideas of the philosophes could have pene-
trated the lower socioeconomic classes, which were still largely illiterate at the time of the French
Revolution. This question has now been set in a new light by Michel Vovelle, "Le Tournant des
mentalités en France 1750–1789: La 'Sensibilité' pré-révolutionnaire," *Social History* 5 (1977):
605–29, who uses statistical data on such variables as demand for postmortem masses, enroll-
ment in religious vocations, contraception, illegitimacy, and child abandonment, to argue for a
major shift in popular attitudes in the period immediately preceding the Revolution, following
lines encouraged by the philosophes.

39. Note the observation of Fouché that in promoting the campaign of de-Christianization
through southern France, he attempted "to substitute the worship of the Republic and natural
morality for the superstitious cults to which the people still unfortunately adhere" (cited in Dawson, *Gods of Revolution*, p. 95). Again, Robespierre, in proposing the cult of the Supreme Being,
stated: "Fanatics, hope for nothing from us. To recall men to the pure cult of the Supreme Being
is to strike a deathblow at fanaticism. All fictions disappear before the truth, and all follies col-
lapse before Reason" (cited in Albert Mathiez, *The Fall of Robespierre* [New York: Alfred Knopf,
1927], p. 101).

40. See Dawson, *Gods of Revolution*, pp. 105ff.; and G. E. Aylmer, "Unbelief in Seventeenth
Century England," in *Puritans and Revolutionaries: Essays in Seventeenth Century History Presented
to Christopher Hill*, ed. D. Pennington and K. Thomas (Oxford: Clarendon Press, 1978), pp.
22–46.

41. Cited in Dawson, *Gods of Revolution*, p. 83.

42. Dawson, *Gods of Revolution*, p. 83. See also such treatments as Albert Soboul, "Jean-Jacques Rousseau et le jacobinisme," *Paysans, sans-culottes et Jacobins* (Paris: Clavreuil, 1966), pp. 257–80; and Alfred Cobban, "The Fundamental Ideas of Robespierre," *Aspects of the French Revolution* (London: Jonathan Cape, 1968), pp. 136–57. The older treatment of Crane Brinton, *The Jacobins* (New York: Macmillan, 1930), esp. pp. 184–222, retains value.

43. See Hodgson, *Order of Assassins*, pp. 9ff., 54–56, 165ff.; Lewis, *The Assassins*, pp. 27ff., 62; and Gelpke, "Geheimbund von Alamut," pp. 287, 292.

44. Lewis, *The Assassins*, pp. 53–55.

45. On the Ghost Dance, see James Mooney, *The Ghost Dance Religion and the Sioux Outbreak of 1890*, ed. A. F. C. Wallace (Chicago: University of Chicago Press, 1965); Leslie Spier, *The Prophet Dance of the Northwest and Its Derivatives*, American Anthropological Association, General Series 1 (1935); Cora Du Bois, *The 1870 Ghost Dance*, University of California Anthropological Records 3 (1939); and W. H. Lindig and A. M. Dauer, "Prophetismus und Geistertanz-Bewegung bei nordamerikanischen Eingeborene," in *Chiliasmus und Nativismus*, ed. Mühlmann, pp. 41–74. Bibliography on the Mau Mau is given above in note 34, and on the Sanusi in note 26, to which must also be added the discussion of Peter Worsley, "The Analysis of Rebellion and Revolution in Modern British Social Anthropology," *Science and Society* 25 (1961): 26–37, esp. pp. 30–33, 37.

46. Naquin, *Millenarian Rebellion in China*, esp. pp. 63–117. On the White Lotus (*Pai-lien chiao*), see Hok-Lam Chan, "The White Lotus-Maitreya Doctrine and Popular Uprisings in Ming and Ch'ing China," *Sinologica* 10 (1969): 211–33; and Daniel Overmyer, *Folk Buddhist Religion* (Cambridge: Harvard University Press, 1976), of which the former is preferable in its assessment of sociopolitical factors.

47. Several of the best books on religions of revolution have been mentioned above: Mooney, *The Ghost Dance;* Hodgson, *Order of Assassins;* Walzer, *Revolution of the Saints;* and Buijtenhuijs, *Le Mouvemement 'Mau-Mau.'* In addition, see Elias Bickerman, *The Maccabees*, trans. Moses Hadas (New York: Schocken, 1947); Franz Michael, *The Taiping Rebellion*, 3 vols. (Seattle: University of Washington Press, 1967); and Paul Clark, *'Hauhau': The Pai Marire Search for Maori Identity* (Auckland: Auckland University Press, 1975). Somewhat disappointing is Rudolf Wagner, *Reenacting the Heavenly Vision: The Role of Religion in the Taiping Rebellion* (Berkeley: Institute of East Asian Studies, 1982).

The Yellow Turban movement is particularly well reported, on which see Henri Maspero, *Le Taoïsme* (Paris: Musée Guimet, 1950); Howard S. Levy, "Yellow Turban Religion and Rebellion at the End of Han," *Journal of the American Oriental Society* 76 (1956): 214–27; Paul Michaud, "The Yellow Turbans," *Monumenta Serica* 17 (1958): 42–127; and R. A. Stein, "Remarques sur les mouvements du taoïsme politico-religieux au IIᵉ siècle après J.C.," *T'oung Pao* 50 (1963): 1–78.

48. E. E. Evans-Pritchard, "Some Collective Expressions of Obscenity in Africa," *The Position of Women in Primitive Societies and Other Essays* (London: Faber & Faber, 1965), pp. 76–101. This category was applied to the Mau Mau oaths by Gluckman, *Order and Rebellion in Tribal Africa*, pp. 137–45; and his analysis remains quite interesting despite the criticisms of Buijtenhuijs, *Le Mouvement 'Mau-Mau,'* pp. 255–99.

49. Pitirim A. Sorokin, *The Sociology of Revolution* (Philadelphia: Lippincott, 1925), pp. 237–69. Sorokin's observations, stripped of their anti-revolutionary bias, have been picked up by Baechler, who argues that in the abandonment of all the norms and appearance of previously taboo practice, revolutions resemble nothing so much as festivals or carnivals (*Revolution*, pp. 7, 40), assessing revolution more as a moment than a process.

50. Roger Bastide, "Messianisme et developpement economique et social," *Cahiers internationaux de sociologie* 31 (1961): 6ff.; Burridge, *New Heaven, New Earth,* pp. 165–68.

51. Dawson, *Gods of Revolution,* p. 95. A similar demonstration, set within the context of the inauguration of a Temple of Reason, is fully described in Philip Dawson, ed., *The French Revolution* (Englewood Cliffs, N.J.: Prentice-Hall, 1967), pp. 121–27, esp. 125. On de-Christianization, see Vovelle, *Religion et révolution,* and on the iconoclastic displays, see Mona Ozouf, *La Fête révolutionnaire 1789–1799* (Paris: Gallimard, 1976), pp. 99–124.

52. For Teng Mou-ch'i, see Muramatsu, "Some Themes in Chinese Rebel Ideologies," p. 260. On the Barcelona exhumations, see Bruce Lincoln, "Revolutionary Exhumations in Spain," *Discourse and the Construction of Society* (New York: Oxford University Press, 1989), pp. 103–27.

53. Danton, cited in Dawson, *Gods of Revolution,* p. 80. Saint-Just, for his part, described the Terror as "the fire of liberty which must purify us as the dross is purged from the molten metal in the furnace," going on to legitimate his proscription of Danton as deriving from quasi-divine inspiration, saying "hitherto it has been assumed that no one would dare to attack famous men, surrounded by a great illusion. . . . I have left all these weaknesses behind me. I have seen nothing but the truth in the universe and I have spoken it" (cited in ibid, pp. 99ff.).

54. Note the fascinating analysis of a Third World coup d'état as ritual action by Edmund Leach, *Culture and Communication* (Cambridge: Cambridge University Press, 1976), pp. 31ff. Although numerous excellent studies of specific iconoclastic episodes exist—e.g., Stephen Gero, *Byzantine Iconoclasm During the Reign of Leo III* (Louvain: Corpus SCO, 1973); or John Phillips, *The Reformation of Images: England 1535–1660* (Berkeley: University of California Press, 1973)— a cross-cultural and synthetic analysis of iconoclasm is sorely needed.

55. See especially the theoretical discussion of Walzer, *Regicide and Revolution,* pp. 1–89. Accounts of the most famous European regicides are to be found in Cicely Veronica Wedgwood, *The Trial of Charles I* (London: Collins, 1964); and Albert Soboul, *Le Procès de Louis XVI* (Paris: Julliard, 1966).

56. Cited in Walzer, *Regicide and Revolution,* p. 4.

57. Ritual vengeance may be taken in turn upon the authors of such "atrocities": Ireton and Cromwell were both exhumed and hanged upon restoration of the monarchy. Chang Chüeh, the leader of the Yellow Turbans, died before the defeat of his movement, only to suffer exhumation, postmortem decapitation, and display of his severed head.

58. Shih, "Some Chinese Rebel Ideologies," p. 172.

59. On Cromwell's consolidation of power after the completion of the civil war, see Austin Woolrich, "Oliver Cromwell and the Rule of the Saints," in *The English Civil War and After,* ed. R. H. Parry (London: Macmillan, 1970), pp. 59–77. On Chu Yüan-chang and the founding of the Ming dynasty, see John W. Dardess, "The Transformation of Messianic Revolt and the Founding of the Ming Dynasty," *Journal of Asian Studies* 29 (1970): 539–58. The founding of the Abbasid dynasty presents a very similar picture within an Islamic context.

On the Ranters, see Cohn, *Pursuit of the Millennium,* pp. 287–330; Hill, *World Turned Upside Down,* pp. 148–93; and A. L. Morton, *The World of the Ranters* (London: Lawrence & Wishart, 1970). The most important literature on the Fifth Monarchists is cited in note 36; that on the Levellers and Diggers is large and well-known.

60. The French Revolution offers some of the clearest examples of this process. See Michel Vovelle, *Les Métamorphoses de la fête en Provence, 1750–1820* (Paris: Flammarion, 1976); A. Aulard, "Les Noms révolutionnaires des communes de France," *Revue de Paris* (Sept.–Oct.

1926): 551–69; and Albert Soboul, "Sentiment religieux et cultes populaires pendant la Révolution: Saintes patriotes et martyrs de la Liberté," *Paysans, sans-culottes et Jacobins,* pp. 183–202. For a parallel development of a revolutionary hagiography, see Ali Mazrui, "On Heroes and Uhuru-Worship," *Transition* 3 (1963): 23–28.

61. The role of the church in Spanish politics during and before the civil war is presented in E. Allison Peers, *Spain, the Church and the Orders* (London: Burns, Oates, and Washbourne, 1945); and Gerald Brenan, *The Spanish Labyrinth* (Cambridge: Cambridge University Press, 1971), pp. 39–55 et passim; as well as the relevant sections of such standard histories as Hugh Thomas, *The Spanish Civil War* (New York: Harper and Row, 1961); Gabriel Jackson, *The Spanish Republic and the Civil War* (Princeton: Princeton University Press, 1965); and Pierre Broué and Émile Témime, *The Revolution and the Civil War in Spain,* trans. T. White (Cambridge: MIT Press, 1970). The nationalist perspective is set forth in Antonio Montero, *Historia de la persecución religiosa en Expaña 1936–1939* (Madrid: Editorial Católica, 1961). Religious dimensions of the anarchists and libertarians are recognized by Brenan, *Spanish Labyrinth,* pp. 188–93; and Hobsbawm, *Primitive Rebels,* pp. 74–92.

62. Balandier, "Messianismes et nationalismes en Afrique Noir," p. 42, and "Phénomenes sociaux totaux et dynamique sociale," *Cahiers internationaux de sociologie* 30 (1961): 23. In particular, Robert Buijtenhuijs has made excellent use of Balandier's position in his study of the Mau Mau. Baechler also presses for a discipline devoted to the total study of revolutionary phenomena, a discipline he dubs "staseology."

63. Baechler, *Revolution,* p. 198n., observes that Delacroix foretold the revolution of 1848 on the basis of declining courtesy on the street and proceeds to suggest that politeness may be "a collection of symbolic gestures evolved by a group to drain off aggression between its members." Alternatively, etiquette may be viewed as the quotidian behavioral manifestations of cultural values, which are abandoned as the system of values breaks down.

64. Cited in Yang, *Religion in Chinese Society,* p. 227. Note the extremely similar statements contained within the Treatise on the Invalidity of the Claim of Muhammad Ahmad, the false Mahdi issued by the Mufti of the Court of Appeal in Khartoum during the Mahdist insurrection:

> Know o brethren, that Allah has arranged things for me and you in such a way that Religion and authority are two inseparable brothers. Religion, then, is the foundation, whereas authority protects it and keeps it erect. Now, that which is not protected will perish and lack support. Therefore, Religion can only exist through authority. . . . If you know all this and also that these glorious verses of the Koran and these magnificent Traditions (hadith) imply that it is obligatory to obey those who have the command and that it is forbidden to fight them and to rebel against them, then you will no doubt be satisfied that he who withdraws from obedience, even if it is only an inch, is rebellious against Allah and will die a heathen.

Cited in Rudolph Peters, *Islam and Colonialism* (The Hague: Mouton, 1979), p. 71.

APPENDIX A

The invocations of §§1–2 are taken from the *Washington Post,* September 28, 2001, p. A18, and reflect passages on the first page of the holograph instructions. This page was subsequently withheld from the general public by the FBI but apparently was available to the *Post* at the time of publication. The *Post* and other American papers published only excerpts from the original text, while on September 30, 2001, the *Observer* published a full translation of the four pages made available by the FBI. §§3–38 are taken from this version, available at www.observer.co.uk/ international/story/0,6903,560773,00.html. The *Observer* lists its translation as having been initially prepared for the *New York Times* by Capital Communications Group, a Washington-based international consulting firm, and by Imad Musa, a translator for the firm. The footnotes supplying references for the Quranic passages quoted in the text are my addition.

1. Sura 8:48.
2. Sura 4:71.
3. Sura 3:136.
4. Sura 2:250, an allusion to the battle of David and Goliath.
5. Sura 3:154.
6. Sura 23:117.
7. Sura 3:167.
8. Sura 3:168.
9. Ibid.
10. Sura 8:50.
11. Sura 9:13.
12. Sura 8:18.
13. Sura 3:200.
14. Sura 8:50.
15. Sura 8:48.
16. Sura 3:141.
17. Sura 8:15.
18. Sura 8:12.
19. Sura 8:78.
20. Sura 87:16–17.
21. Sura 2:149.
22. Sura 33:22.

APPENDIX B

1. Text from the *New York Times*, Monday, October 8, 2001, p. B6. Also available at www.whitehouse.gov/news/releases/2001/10/20011007-8.html.

APPENDIX C

1. Translated text taken from the *New York Times*, Monday, October 8, 2001, p. B7. Another version available at www.cnn.com/2001/WORLD/asiapcf/central/10/07/ret.binladen.transcript/index.html.

APPENDIX D

Taken from, www.pfaw.org/issues/right/robertson_falwell.html, with minor changes in punctuation and spelling.

1. This intervention seems so bizarre to the untutored reader that it begs for explanation. It follows directly on the passage in which Jerry Falwell cites II Chronicles 7:14 and states "there's

not much we can do in the Church but what we're supposed to do, and that is pray" (§6). Pat Robertson here reminds his colleague that there is a second practice that they and many of their fellow evangelists also recognize as a necessary part of the repentance enjoined by that verse, even though it is not explicitly mentioned in the biblical text. Here he relies on a line of analysis advanced by Bill Bright, president of the Campus Crusade for Christ, who has argued for many years that fasts, especially those of forty days' duration, are the only practice that meet all conditions of the self-humbling required by II Chronicles 7:14. Both Falwell and Robertson have participated in well-publicized fasts with Bright, who has expressed his views in numerous, rather repetitive books, including *The Coming Revival: America's Call to Fast, Pray, and "Seek God's Face"* (Orlando: New Life Publications, 1995), or *The Transforming Power of Fasting and Prayer* (Orlando: New Life Publications, 1997).

   2. This phrase, which recurs at §16, designates the kind of self-humbling that goes with profound repentance, as described in II Chronicles 7:14. As such, it marks the sincere contrition that is a necessary prelude to spiritual revival.